With a Flower

upon the

Ocean

First Published 2004 by Countyvise Limited, 14 Appin Road, Birkenhead, Wirral CH41 9HH in conjunction with the author Edward T. Wilkins.

British Library Cataloguing in Publication Data.
A catalogue record for this book is available from the British Library.

ISBN 1 901231 44 5

The Memoirs of a Man dressed as a Matelot in World War Two

by

Edward T. Wilkins

THE COLUMBINE STORY

Researched and written by   Edward T. Wilkins

Compositor and Designer   Edward B. Wilkins

Proof Reader   Irene C. Wilkins

Laid originally in Times New Roman, Point 12
at
Brierfield Road Liverpool
2003.

This edition laid in Square721 BT, Point 10.

Dedication

This book would not have been written without the initial enthusiasm for the idea shown by Edmund Gander when escorting a Columbine Reunion Party around the '*S. S. Great Britain*' in Bristol some years ago, the '*magnamatiousness*' of Mrs Alfie Turner in giving me sight of personal letters from her husband, many suggestions about research from Jack Lavis, and Ed Maguire, but more than anything else, the astonishing memory of my very dear friend Ted Lamont supplying such a cornucopia of information and anecdote. Many others have contributed to the sum total of anecdote contained within these pages to whom I must express deep thanks in the hope that the dialogue attributed to those various occasions though sometimes fictitious in structure will be agreed by the participants or protagonists as being true in substance. The whole has been a labour of love in remembrance of a time in my life though of short duration has been of inestimable value, and I dedicate this volume to every man-jack who ever sailed in corvettes, with a particular salute to those lower-deck 'Hostilities Only' who served with me in K.94

TO THE MEN OF COLUMBINE

Across those green amazing seas
To and fro grey sheep-dogs raced and crept.
Made of iron tho - not flesh, these dogs of War;
Yet crewed by men and driven there
By Britain's reasonable steam.

Upon that mighty watery deep
They did not sleep
Until the U-boat wolf-packs
From those seas they swept . . .
And many wept.
And we know it's not all been done or said:
Not enough to praise their grim and dangerous work
In foulest storms and ice-slicked decks,
Broken hearts and broken necks
Torpedo bait and condor prey
Through threats that laced each night and day

The convoys ran the flaming gauntlet,
Kept the home-fires burning; Zig-zagging and returning-
Grey sheep-dogs turning
War's bloody tide at last to victory.
And, me? The son of a hero who went with you to fight
Demonic forces of the Nazi war machine in all its might.
And I know what you did,
The time you bought for the todays we now enjoy.
And this feeling isn't hidden-
For a little of your honour is also mine
Thanks to you all present and correct, the Men of Columbine

Edward Blair Wilkins, 1999

Foreword

By way of explanation: My father-in-law was a 1914 to 1919 Naval Rating serving in the Fleet Reserve when 'called to the colours' for the Second World War. He often spoke of his early years in *'The Andrew'* when (as he put it) 'I did my time in the Service when the ships were just finished being carved from wood and the men made of iron!' The inference was patently obvious. He re-classified all Hostilities Only conscripts as mere 'Men Dressed As' with probably more truth than he realised.

But we did our best.

The Man Dressed As

Introduction

There is, I suppose, some precedent for my decision to put on record the following history. In 1951 Nicholas Monsarrat published a novel entitled 'The Cruel Sea', alleging to be an account of the exploits of a small group of men and two small ships in World War Two, and such was its epic nature it seized public imagination, almost immediately being made into a very successful film; indeed, to my mind, one of the best sea adventures ever produced.

H. M. S. Columbine K.94

It centred upon a new type of Escort Vessel called a Corvette that Monsarrat named **Compass Rose** to which he allocated the Pendant Number K.49. My interest was aroused on realising this number was the reverse of that carried by my ship, H.M.S. Columbine, K.94.

These small craft, put together with such haste to meet urgent need in 1940-1945 were, by 1952 almost totally non-existent although only thirty-three were sunk or damaged during the war; the survivors were sold and broken up with such alacrity that the film makers were hard put to find a suitable vessel.

Columbine was under a Norwegian flag, her name changed to **Leif Welding** doing work as a whaler in Antarctic waters, so **Coreopsis** K.32 was returned from Greece and her pendant number altered to K.49 to become a film star complemented by characters in the words of the author, 'wholly fictitious'. In comparison ALL the individuals mentioned in the following account actually said or played out the actions attributed to them, one particular factual observation assisting my resolve to write yet another facet of the corvette saga being a divergence from Monsarrat's title and made by Lt. A.L. Turner the first Commanding Officer of K.94:

'Although it is true that all who went down to the sea in ships during the war years had hardships and unpleasant experiences, on occasion they also enjoyed periods when, in spite of the enemy, it was good to be alive and at sea.'

It was during 1939 as First Lord of the Admiralty that Winston Churchill became increasingly conscious of the probability of U-boat attacks becoming greater toward the end of 1940 when the German admiral Doenitz would have a preponderance of this kind of weapon, so he prescribed that all work on large vessels which could not come into service before the end of that year be halted in favour of types capable of getting built within twelve or even, eight months. He had in mind of course vessels, which could be deployed against the U-boats in Home Waters thus leaving the larger and more lethal destroyers to range the oceans. In a minute to his naval colleagues he wrote:

'It ought to be possible to design destroyers which can be completed in under a year, in which case fifty at the very least should be begun forthwith ... the arrival in our

fleets of fifty of these medium emergency types I am contemplating would liberate all larger vessels for ocean work and combat.'

Orders for twenty-six of these were placed on the 25th July 1939 and a further thirty on August 31st when Job Number J.6067 was allocated to the Albion Dockyard at Bristol, work beginning on the 22nd October as the British faced a series of naval disasters rocking confidence in their beliefs of impregnability.

In the same way that the collapse of the Maginot Line had proved an ineffectual defence for the French, so the audacious attack on the 14th October by Lt. Gunter Prien in U.47, sinking the **Royal Oak** within the 'safe anchorage' of Scapa Flow demonstrated the sterility of thought in that direction as well. Then, on the 23rd November the armed merchant cruiser **Rawalpindi** with her four out-dated six inch guns fought a suicidal battle against the battle-cruisers **Scharnhorst** and **Gneisenau** and on December the fourth the battleship **Nelson** was mined as she entered Loch Ewe. There was momentary respite and jubilation at the news of the action off the River Plate (South America) when Captain Langsdorff scuttled the **Graf Spee**, and, later, on February 1940 when Vian in **H.M.S.Cossack** intercepted the auxiliary of the **Spee**, the **Altmark**, releasing two hundred and ninety-nine prisoners. When Germany invaded Norway by dispatching the **Scharnhorst** and **Gneisenau**, supported by ten destroyers to Narvic in the April of that year, the Admiralty sent Chief Engine Room Artificer Robert Makepiece Bains to Bristol where his tact and acquisitive promptings probably brought J.6067 painstakingly to completion, and three months later he was joined by the ship's first Commanding Officer, and a week after that came Collings the First Lieutenant, Trew the Navigator, Ridley the Coxswain and other key ratings.

The vessel was launched on the 13th August 1940 and shifted the same day to Cardiff to ship main engines and boilers which were installed by Richardson Westgarth & Clark, some wag afterwards suggested sounded like a firm of solicitors, particularly when the ship ran into rough weather.

On 8th October she raised steam, and as the fag-end of that summer gutted out in the fog of 12th October, the lorries containing the main draft arrived at Bristol to discharge a vociferous and curious mixture of Active Service and Hostilities Only ratings brought together in a common need but as yet intolerant of each other's ability. One of these stood in the rear of a vehicle heaving off kit-bags and hammocks with a total disregard to their destination as forty year old Chief Petty Officer Peter Ridley, senior rating of the Lower Deck, walked amid youthful pandemonium gaining a semblance of order. Suddenly, a heavy kit bag dropped into a dirty rain puddle flecked with oil at his feet and splashed him from cap to boot. The banter ceased, smiles appeared and disappeared as he snarled: 'Who did that! What man did that?'

The seaman, who had served previously on the battleship Rodney, leapt from the tailboard and saluted the Cox'n with studied efficiency: 'Able Seaman Troops sir' he said, 'trained man'.

A look passed between the two, a warning of future disciplinary action as they filed aboard, this company of conscripts and volunteers. Stoker Petty Officers Spud Murphy and Ted Witts, the Yeoman of Signals McCarthy, Leading Telegraphist 'Doc' Rowlands, Officer's Cook Frank Milton, Stewards Peppin and Baker, Buffer Granville, the Asdic Team of Setherton Molloy and Nuttall . . . seamen and communicators, a total of four officers and fifty ratings drawn mainly from the Devonport Division; and once aboard, the Hostilities Only contingent accepted their quarters without demur unaware of naval protocol. Far different was the reaction of others who were flabbergasted at the way stokers and seamen, communicators and; 'tiffies' were crowded together in the forecastle mess decks, a space difficult enough to move in without blundering into a stanchion or another body. The area immediately below the upper deck forward of the four inch gun was about six hundred square feet, i.e., 22 x 30 feet having six mess tables at which they were to eat and, when occasion permitted, relax. The Petty Officers had their accommodation aft while the Officers shared cabins and a Wardroom mid-ships below the Bridge.

The ship was, as previously stated, of small proportion, in fact, just 203 feet overall in length, 33ft 5ins wide maximum which differed from standard by those odd inches, and had a displacement of 940 tons. She was equipped with two cylindrical boilers serving a four-cylinder vertical triple-expansion engine developing 2750 i.h.p. Feeding a single screw capable of driving the vessel to maximum speed of sixteen knots. She was fitted with a four inch gun circa 1917 on the fo'c'sle, a .303 Hotchkiss gun mounted on each arm of the Bridge, a single two pounder pom-pom mid-ships, and a couple of Lewis machine guns provided more for morale than for any damage they might inflict. The mast, contrary to naval practice, was erected in front of the Bridge below which was a well deck; this mast removed and placed abaft the Bridge during a subsequent re-fit. Two depth charge throwers were sited in both port and starboard waists for ejection over each gun-whale while together with charges rolled off the stern would create the 'pattern' to enclose any lurking U-boat. Supplementing those held in readiness was a complete stowage for forty of these explosive drums.

A minute from Churchill to the Controller on the 25th February 1940 said:

'I should like the word destroyer to cover ships formerly described as fast escort vessels which are, in fact medium destroyers. I do not like the word whaler which is an entire misnomer as they are certainly not going to catch whales'

Thus did J.6067, a ship of 940 tons with a width as I have mentioned - some five and a half inches greater than the laid down standard, and depth charges bristling a broad whalers stern came into being as a corvette and along with all her sisters in the class, was named after a flower. She swung round calibrating compasses on the 23rd, commissioned on the 24th as H.M.S. Columbine K.94, and after twelve months and seven days work by Charles Hill and Company was on the 29th October 1940 handed over to Lt. Alfred Lawrence Turner R.N.R.

Mrs Alan William Peck, wife of the director and chief naval architect of the firm responsible for the building of Yard 279 and of eight Flower Class Corvettes, wrote a poem for each as they came off the stocks. Here is the second of her thoughts to go to sea in the Ward-room of K.94. I can think of no better honour or preface to this history of our sturdy little ship built with such outstanding loyalty to the war effort, by some of the 60 women and 1350 men employed at the Albion yard: -

Ship shaped and Bristol fashioned Columbine,
Unlike thy namesake of the summer breeze
That gaily dances on a slender stem
And catches every passing glance to please,
Thou'rt made of sterner stuff:
Thou'rt built to deal
With storm and gun, torpedo bomb and mine,
And all the lurking dangers of the deep.
God guide the men who man thee, Columbine.
What priceless things you stand for Columbine:
The treasures of the world are nought to these:
That little folk may unmolested go
Across the waters of the seven seas.
That freedom justice, brotherhood prevail
In happy homes, in every land and clime.
To live for, fight for, die for, God inspire
To victory dauntless Columbine.

AWP 1940

Chapter 1

A preliminary instruction on four inch gun drill was carried out on board by the Naval Instructor from Avonmouth and a party of ten ratings sent to the base for general guidance on the use of the Hotchkiss .303 machine guns, and that evening the Gun Layer Tommy Carr walked alongside the ship impressing every detail he could into his memory for it was in his mind to construct a wooden model of this vessel which was now his home. On Friday 27th September when he had come to see the ship, or rather the number to which he'd been drafted, J 6067, he had found her with half the upper deck incomplete and no funnel. The town was subject to air raids, and his mother's family living close by, he had decided to grant himself weekend leave after having a few words with Chiefy Bains and with Ridley who had assured him that 'a period of two hours work a day would prove sufficient'.

Lt. Ed Maguire watched as the rating walked through the melee of dock-yard mateys and their gear on the quay-side wondering if it was queasiness or unease causing the up and down perambulation of the man because he himself was plagued with some doubt as to his ability to survive amicably with his new companions. His pay, as a Royal Canadian Volunteer Reserve Lieutenant was greater he reflected, than the Commanding Officer of this ship he'd just joined, and that was one hell of a problem. Turner didn't appear to be the sort of guy who'd allow that sort a thing to become an irritation but it was early days yet. His experience had created a caution in an otherwise nonchalant attitude to life when he discovered that fellow officers regarded him as a junior Rothschild and either stood away embarrassed or expected him to lash out with the dollars. He grinned suddenly, thinking of his recent call on the famous wine merchant of Bristol, Harvey's, when in a moment of excess he'd invested . . . yes that's the word he thought . . .invested in quite a large quantity of booze for the Wardroom which was now located in the two-pounder magazine below the Bridge. Tidily stowed next to shot and shell it was probably the most lethal merchandise in the flat opposite the rum locker and if Colonel Chin-strap could escape from the new Tommy Handley series of I.T.M.A. to find the K.94 hoard, he'd never return to the sobriety of the B.B.C he was sure of that. 'I don't mind if I do Sir' he mimicked passing the new Yeoman of Signals who gaped open mouthed as he went by.

Percy Drewry had also just come aboard, a hurried appointment in place of the unfortunate McCarthy who had fallen down a ladder to injure his spine, and he scratched his head on hearing the transatlantic twang. 'Crikey, Yanks and Kiwis, I wonder if Hitler knows what he's up against?' he muttered. Percy had been introduced to his staff, Ordinary Signalman Holland, Ordinary Signalman McCall, and Trained Operator Wheeler RNZVR whose stylised vocabulary already had him thinking in terms of a Maori/English dictionary. He shrugged, sighed and followed the lieutenant below deck to his own quarters.

The passage north was one of foul weather during which was found a wallowing merchantman in the Minches and an offer made to take her in tow. After ensuring her safety Columbine disengaged. Proceeding on her way as the weather rapidly deteriorated causing Turner to determine in the increasing dark to steer his ship gently round a Point into the haven of a small Sound spotted on the chart. The gale was screaming all around except in the Sound where it was as calm as the proverbial duck-pond and an anchor was dropped well toward the southern end where high land to the westward gave ample shelter. 'Keep an Officer's Watch, Number One' he said, 'and maintain steam. Let me know at once if the gale shifts into the North'. The Sound was open to the sea at this point and he knew that such a change would put Columbine off a lee shore with a probable heavy sea. He was awakened just before midnight by the urgent voice of the O.O.W.

'Wake up Sir! There's hell to pay on deck!'

'What's wrong Maguire?'

'The wind's shifted to the North Sir. It's blowing and snowing like the devil and the ship's all over the joint!'

As Turner struggled into his duffel coat clambering up the ladder and passing through the wheel-house he ordered one man to ring 'Stand-by Engines' on the engine room telegraph and sent another to call the coxswain up to the wheel then stepped from the wheel-house into a screaming black inferno in which he could dimly see the occasional flash of a wave-crest roaring by close alongside the ship, the raging blizzard reducing visibility to less than ten yards. When he got to the open Bridge he saw that Columbine was lying at an angle of forty-five degrees from her cable, which meant she was across the seas, which were high and breaking. She was rolling heavily; and shipping a great deal of water to windward and the possibility of dragging the anchor was very real.

He bent to a voice pipe, ' Who's that on the wheel?'

'Ridley, Sir'

'Good man. Slow ahead and hard a starboard'.

Slowly - so slowly - degree by degree, the ship began to come round and ride to her anchor more easily but even so, from time to time a heavier squall would howl down and losing all the ground made, she would roll and plunge furiously, driven forward by her engines.

After a particularly heavy squall when she was back into a position almost beam-on to the wind and sea, the snow stopped, Suddenly, as though a curtain had been drawn back; but the wind was as fierce as ever and the clearer visibility turned Alfie's blood cold in a way which had nothing to do with the temperature. As he strained his eyes into that surrounding dark he could dimly make out a huge black cliff barely a hundred yards away with seas smashing at its base and bursting halfway up its three hundred foot face. Only the fiercely churning whiteness of the breaking waters enabled him to see it at all and he realised his ship was dragging its anchor, bearing down to destruction, knowing, that if she struck that iron cliff which had deep water at its steep base, no-one, not one soul would escape.

He saw that the First Lieutenant had come top-side and shouted above the screaming wind 'Have all hands mustered on deck with life-belts on Number One' then, gripping a voice-pipe, 'Full speed ahead, helm hard to starboard' he ordered, praying the vessel would steady into the eye of the wind and allow her to drive for awhile as the situation grew in his thoughts with daunting proportions. If the weather conditions had been his only concern he could have borne them with equanimity as he'd done many times before, but the situation confronting him at this time also bespoke the hazard of rocks and the closeness of the Sound in which he was trapped . . . a bare three miles wide, twice that distance from North to South, and until an abatement in the weather confined within these bounds.

There was no means of estimating the depth of water beneath them at any time, the steep seas made Columbine's movements so violent that the consequent 'quenching' under her keel rendered her Asdic-Set inoperative. So he stood there, half frozen and a prey to every sort of doubt and fear which extreme responsibility can bring. Everything depended on his decisions alone he knew, and he was conscious of the isolation of spirit, which every sea captain feels at times, through the very nature of his job.

He again called to his First Lieutenant: 'Will you try to make your way forward Number One, and let me know in which direction the anchor cable is leading!'

'Aye Aye Sir' he replied manfully and immediately put himself at risk, crawling on hands and knees along the foc'sle-head as the wind rose to hurricane force, his powerful torch unable to pierce the murk to the hawse-pipe. Four times he made that perilous journey, each time the engines were slowed to make things easier, but all he could report was that the chain was jumping and vibrating like a mad thing when he put his hand on the length between the windlass and the bows. As he had picked his way back to the Bridge for the fourth time clinging to the life-lines the seamen had rigged for his safety, he had prayed, 'Oh God, don't let him ask me to try again' and now felt Alfie's torch-light warming his face, and heard his C.O. exclaim, 'Heavens Number One, you look terrible! Look, get yourself down by the asdic set . . . I'll send for some hot coffee - that'll warm you up'.

The coffee when it came to the Bridge was steaming hot and satisfyingly strong, tasting even better after Turner had laced it with a stiff tot of brandy, and when he saw the beneficial effect it was having on his officer, he repeated the dose on himself with equal result, but had to guard against the possible smothering of his brain by the strong alcohol . . . like mental cotton wool . . . which would create a certain lethargy in its wake.

The crew, with the exception of those needed to work the ship, were huddled on the engine-room casing abaft the Bridge as being the safest, and certainly the warmest place on deck. And the see-saw went on and on back and forth until it was impossible to judge the position of the ship in the remotest degree and would have occasioned no surprise if at any time during the night a grinding crash would signal the end of Columbine on one of the myriad rocks lying in wait for her, until, at long last the first pale streaks of dawn began to show dimly as the snow slackened. Wiping away the salt from beneath smarting eyelids Alfie was able to discern the uncertain outline of a bold bluff and recognised it as the headland rounded the previous evening and knew their ordeal was over. A bearing or two indicated that K.94 was lying in the middle of the channel leading out to sea, and as though conscious that it had done its worst and lost, the snow ceased and within a few minutes an island surmounted by an unlighted light-house came into view. They were safe.

Maguire grinned wanly, glancing around the Bridge, and allowing his eyes to wander over the Sound. 'Good God Sir, how the heck did we do it?' But Turner did not answer him, he was thinking of the inadequacy of Man and questioning whether it was Poseidon or Neptune, or God Himself who had shown them His power; and, later, when orders were given to hove-short the anchor chain and the cable came in over the windlass it was observed that the rocks had polished the last thirty fathoms of it so effectively that it looked like a giant's silver watch chain, with the anchor itself remarkably like a Gold Albert. It seemed as though the gods had given Columbine a token of their protection and she steamed into Tobermory on the 25th November fearing nothing.

The following day she was out drilling the gun crews under the supervision of members from the staff of Commodore 'Monkey' Stephenson who had, by this time secured a reputation as a holy terror and a scourge to any inefficiency; and ships had to pass these tests of seamanship, gunnery, signals, and the like in the same way Boy Scouts win proficiency medals, and there was no 'passing out' until the Admiral was satisfied nothing better could be achieved. During one day's practice, on the 27th November it was, the supply party was drilled and found to be deficient in number in the Shell Room, so a Coder was sent down there. They passed the test, but whether the Communication rating would be employed this way during actual engagement with enemy would be another matter.

Another episode loosely connected to ordnance, occurred when Stephenson sent his Gunnery Officer, a 'pusser' fellow steeped in the age-old conceptions of the Royal Navy. He was totally impervious to any persuasion by Lt. Maguire to steer him away aft to see the Depth Charges.

'Ridiculous things' he grunted, 'clumsy and mostly ineffectual devices' and pronounced his higher-ranking verdict that the war at sea would be won by naval gunfire.

'That's right Lieutenant - gunfire. And now I'd like you to take me down to the magazine'.

'The magazine Sir?'

'The magazine; I've come aboard to inspect the magazine'

'But Sir, you've seen the guns . . . It's only . . .'

'Lieutenant - its my job to ensure that all ships of the Royal Navy, and I'm fairly certain this is one of them, have correct stowage of their ammunition. Please conduct me to your magazine'.

Maguire stepped into the Wardroom and picked up the necessary keys, throwing an agonised look towards Number One sitting with the Confidential Books but that worthy studiously kept his eyes on those secrets betwixt leaded covers. 'You're on your own Ed' thought the luckless Canadian.

The magazine door was thrown open and for a moment the world ended. An oath which would have appalled the First Lord of the Admiralty had he known Naval Officers capable of such Lower Deck exaggeration, pulled Maguire into the room faster than a stone leaving a sling-shot to stand before the irate emissary from Rear Admiral Stephenson whose face was changing slowly from puce to a near normal pallor.

'In my entire career in the Navy, the BRITISH Navy Lieutenant, I have never been witness to such as this. Booze Sir, I refer to these cases of whisky and whatnot stowed amongst ordnance supplies. Damn it man, it's practically sacrilegious; does your Captain know about it?' Maguire decided quickly, 'No Sir, my responsibility entirely Sir'

'Very well. Get the stuff out of here pronto, chop chop and all that, and I shall ignore this relapse. Columbine's putting on a good show so far, I wouldn't like to spoil it for the rest of the chaps. But get things ship-shape down here eh? Ship-shape and Bristol fashioned as on the ship's plaque right? Pity there isn't a Bristol in Canada. Get on with it boy'.

The ex-barrack stanchion heaved himself up the ladder and off Columbine to a whistle of relief from his victim . . . er, from behind a closed fist. At last the mock alarms ceased and Columbine sailed down to Liverpool where, on the 9th December 1940 she became attached to the 6th Escort Group.

Turner fell sick with tonsillitis on the 12th December and the ship took on a temporary skipper, Lt. Sayers, a reticent sort of fellow who had of necessity to rely a great deal on the officers and men of his new command and they, in turn almost totally unprepared for the kind of life upon which they now embarked; sailing in convoy westbound out of the Clyde. The episode in the Sound had been full of apprehension, and at times perched on the razor-edge of Turner's deliberations, but the Naval Regulars had never served in such a vessel on convoy duties. For most of the conscripted men it was their first experience of an ocean in **any** ship. One or two had served a few weeks in small craft but not corvettes, so their chief preoccupation during that baptism was to curse the 'dry land sailors' at the drafting office who had allocated them to this 'gyrating one-funnelled bastard' lurching over and through the Atlantic swell with mess-decks awash, with food, when it came from the galley aft cold and saturated with the salty tang of the spray as it whipped over the gun-whale to surprise the cook-of-the-mess struggling to maintain balance in the Port waist; trying to judge the arrival of the next 'greenie' before running either up or down to the security of the short fo'c's'le.

Anything between decks not properly fastened soon found itself sloshed about in six or more inches of water, battered against one bulkhead, spun round by a stanchion and rammed against another bulkhead ad infinitum. Before the war men serving in destroyers and smaller craft were given what was termed 'Hard Lying Money' to compensate for inconvenient living quarters, but this to the new-comers was 'bloody ridiculous'. With the clothing lockers steeped to the hinges in a mixture of sea water and vomit, no financial emolument could compensate for the agony of those on the upper deck coming saturated from their watch to find no warm clothing to still their shivering. Small wonder then that tempers ran high and bickering broke loose among the polyglot conscripts: Cockneys, Geordies, Scousers, Jocks and Taffies. Stokers coming off watch would immediately appropriate the three wash basins in the bath-room as of right much to the audible annoyance of other watch-keepers compelled by necessity to perform their ablutions in such a restricted and impersonal area, but in course of time snobbery or caste vanished in the Lower Deck as if thought had been severed at the cervical vertebrae, the entire ship finding a safer and more profitable breakwater in new-found feelings of tolerance and later, admiration. Or as Able Seaman Albert Troops observed succinctly 'We're all bastards, and we're all in the **same** bloody bastard'.

Outside, the merchantmen ploughed on at a steady six knots, spread over the ocean in ranks like the Coldstreams or the Grenadiers on Horse-guards Parade, impressive in their utter disregard of vulnerability; hopeful in their complete confidence in the British Navy.

Chapter 2

On December 20th Escorts received the standard signal from the Commodore that he was prepared to disband the convoy to proceed independently, normal practice when reaching the designated longitude and latitude south of Iceland. Toward evening, dark but with sea moderate, the Senior Officer of Escorts determined that it would be opportune to exercise his ships in Fleet manoeuvres and promulgated the signal Blue 90. The ships were in line abreast and the signal involved a simultaneous turn of ninety degrees to starboard. Misinterpreted as a turn to port by the Watch, Columbine, and the ship on her port beam, the sloop Aberdeen, on receipt of the 'Executive' turned in toward one another at a combined speed of thirty knots. Aberdeen crammed on extra revolutions in order to surge past Columbine's bows but distance defeated this ploy and a brilliant flash lit up the darkness as steel rasped against steel while astonished indeed terrified Bridge personnel gaped as Columbine seemed to climb over the stern of the sloop scattering her depth-charges in all directions.

Ed Maguire had come from the 'Middle' and had turned in for about two hours when he was all but thrown out of his bunk by the impact. He jumped into his trousers, hastily pulled a jumper over his shoulders and headed for the Bridge, passing 'Bagsy' Baker standing with his hand up to his nose, and enquired if the steward had been hurt.

'Not much Sir, got thrown up against that blessed bulkhead there. What's happened d'you think Sir?'

'Don't know. Going to find out.'

Getting to the upper deck he noticed some ratings preparing their one and only life-boat and had visions of going for an uncomfortably cold swim.

Cdr. Sayers was on the Bridge when he got there, the ships had parted and were lying still in the water. The Aberdeen seemed to have sustained only superficial damage (except to the C.O's pride if any credibility could be placed on remarks coming from her loud-hailer) but Sayers was of the opinion that his ship had been damaged as far back as the forward bulkhead.

Ed thought about this then ventured:
'Would it not be policy to kinda, shore this up, strengthen it Sir?'

Sayers looked up bleakly, 'Certainly. Go ahead with it will you Lieutenant.'

Making his way forward Maguire could hear the sounds of singing and general hilarity and was completely astounded by the merriment he found in the mess deck because he had thoughts of a cold swim still in his mind.

'What on earth is all the noise about?' he demanded irritably and was greeted by a chorus:
'We'll all get leave out of this Sir!

Soberly he looked into one face after another and the racket settled, and in the quietness said deliberately, 'I want some of you to assist me in making the forward bulk-head stronger because I think there's nothing . . . but sea on the other side of it'

Someone coughed nervously, one or two others put ears to the partition, slowly nodding heads, licking lips suddenly gone dry as they realised that had that bulk-head not held the seas would have washed through Columbine and she would have been literally swallowed in one mighty gulp!

Indeed it was also very fortunate that they were in a calm sea which enabled them to make two or three knots under their own power, though it being necessary to protect them from the enemy, the destroyer **Wolverine** was detailed to escort them to land-fall when they arrived on Christmas Morning on a calm and sunny day to enjoy the amenities of the Royal Hotel Stornaway. A somewhat two-edged benefaction because the following day the ship was boarded by the local constabulary in the form of one Inspector, one Sergeant plus two Constables bearing a written complaint from The Royal. Something to do with missing cutlery, and 'could they be assured that it had not been borrowed by the Columbine crew?

The indignant Sayers was loath to accept this unprecedented assault on his ship but Chiefy Bains and Ridley advised him to co-operate and a search was conducted first in the forward mess-decks then aft; nothing was found except suspicion.

A day or two later Columbine cast off to proceed to Scapa Flow and was placed in dry dock at Lyness on the 28th but was almost immediately shifted from there because a damaged Fleet destroyer from the North Sea area arrived soon after to be 'dished up' in her place. So she finally staggered down to the Tyne where Alfie Turner, recovering from a month with tonsillitis relieved Sayers from his temporary command on the 13th January 1941.

There they remained for three months as repairs were effected and because the bows needed a great deal of attention it was decided to lengthen the short fo'c's'le bringing it to a point abreast the Bridge tier and by this means giving extra accommodation below decks. This was to conform to the latest designs but however was not made effective until a few months later in Tilbury. Leave, extended leave was granted to each watch in turn and on March 7th the 'buzz' was heard that the **Royal Oak** and other ill-fated ships had been avenged. Lt.Gunther Prien had gone down in U47, sunk by the conjoined forces of the V&W destroyer **Wolverine** (she who had offered Columbine a tow after the collision with Aberdeen) and the corvettes **Arbutus** and **Camellia.** Luckily no-one could tell at this moment the fate of the little **Arbutus,** or the part Columbine herself was to play in her destiny, but on that day, March 7th 1941 the cheers of the nation was balm to the discomfort of all those small ship sailors. Providing fresh impetus and fresh hope of victory when spring and summer conditions in the North Atlantic would give them a chance to prove their metal.

The ship was in all respects ready for sea on April the First when Leading Telegraphist Eric Lionel Davis arrived at the quayside. He had entered the Royal Navy as a Boy Telegraphist some years previously at H.M.S.Ganges, Shotley, and as he stood looking at the tiny vessel his kit-bag slid from his shoulder; his thoughts erratic, incredulous even, his eyes wandering in seconds from bow to stern. The antique gun on the forecastle, the mini trawler-style box Bridge, and the pom-pom and after carley float seemed enclosed within the dimensions either of a toy or a working model.

'This isn't a naval ship' he frowned in dismay, 'Why haven't I been drafted to a destroyer or cruiser. I'm a trained Naval rating!' his thoughts interrupted at that moment by a shout from the top of the gangway where quartermaster Irvine Phillips kept meticulous watch.

'Hey, you down there', the Q.M. bellowed, 'You the new communication rating? You'd better come aboard chop chop an' get yer gear stowed pretty nifty. We're pushing off in a couple of hours mate'.

Davis shouldered his kit bag once more to climb the sloping gangway, reaching the side of Phillips as an attractive woman escorted by an R.N.R. Lieutenant stopped to smile as she descended to the quayside.

He stiffened to a salute and Turner murmured, 'Arrived in time then? Welcome aboard' returned the salute and moved away.

Eric gestured toward the figure now lost to sight amid dockside buildings, 'She the skipper's missus?'

Irvine grinned, 'Yeh. Just been fixing Alfie's ticklers. Bagsy the steward said he saw her sitting in the captain's cabin with a dirty great big pile of tobacco in front of her and rolling fags by the thousand ready for the voyage.' His grin widened, 'Comes with being married a long time I reckon, crikey, I can't see my party doing it for me.'

Polly Turner walked slowly and thoughtfully past unseen sheds and toiling workmen, reaching her hotel feeling lost and alone. She had bade farewell to her husband not knowing where he might be going nor for how long this new separation might last and felt an urge to do something, to contribute toward the crucial event shaping her life this day. So she went back to the promenade not far from the dockyard where she leaned over the railings looking along the line of coast to the mouth of the Tyne watching and waiting.

Then suddenly Columbine appeared; out from the narrow river, plunging into the wintry rockers of the North Sea. Such a gallant little ship she looked, with the spray bursting over her bows as she steadfastly went toward her business of helping to protect our shipping and our shores.

So she stood there, forlornly, waving a handkerchief though she knew it could not be seen until she heard a voice close by. She looked round, and there was an old chap, also leaning on the railing, watching, like she was - he said, 'Is HE in that ship?'

She smiled at him and replied, 'Yes. He is.' 'Ah - God bless him' the old man said and she went away, warmed and comforted.

The passage from North Shields was an extremely uncomfortable one, particularly in the North Sea and Pentland Firth when almost all the crew were sea-sick - including such old stagers as Coxswain Ridley and Bosun's Mate Glanville. For Leading Telegraphist Davis it was close to nightmare remembered many years later in the lines:

> 'Twas All Fools Day '41 that I joined her
> In North Shields just ere she sailed;
> I looked at the size of the vessel
> And I'm sure that I visibly paled.
> I didn't think she'd ever make it
> Across the Atlantic and back;
> She looked just like a steel coffin,
> By golly the outlook was black.
> I shouldered my kit-bag and hammock
> And carried them over the brow.
> I felt my stomach was sinking
> And I wished I hadn't joined now.
> We sailed on a convoy that evening
> And blimey, wasn't it rough!
> I soon had my head in a bucket
> And found I wasn't so tough.
> I couldn't have cared if the ship sank
> And inwardly cried for my Mum.

Four days later a mysterious change to orders brought the ship into Loch Ewe where the pale and wan visaged crew, shivering with the fresh North-easterly cutting through duffle and hood of those on watch, gained respite and a good night's sleep sheltered by snow covered mountains, next morning continuing through the Kyles to reach Greenock on the fifth of April and to take on board two crates. One contained an outboard motor; the other sent a 'buzz' throughout the ship.

... The passage from North Shields was an extremely uncomfortable ...

... Here the weather broke and all hell was let loose ...

It was a refrigerator, and quite the largest anyone present had ever seen except those used in barracks, causing the 'Jack Dusty' Supply Assistant Pat McCarthy waiting in the starboard waist, to murmur dryly to Ridley,'It's for iced lime juice maybe, when we run short of rum, eh 'Swain?' And the rumour ran straight down the keel to inform the officers that Columbine was destined for the tropics. Another item came on board shortly after, but in a manner admitting to skulduggery. It was a second signal projector.

The idea had been germinating in the mind of Percy Drewry since arriving at Greenock and the addition of a couple of pints under the belt during their run ashore one evening prompted him to say, 'Y'know Chesty, I reckon I've thought of a way to make life easier for you on the Bridge.'

'What d'you mean?' asked Wheeler.

'You could get yourself another ten inch signal lamp,'

As they sauntered along the jetty the couple came within the shadow of a loading shed. Inconspicuously easing himself the Trained Operator mumbled fruitfully, 'And how in the hell . . . d'you . . . imagine . . . I can get a bloody spare ten inch projector, eh?' Then grinned as his companion jerked a thumb at the corvette **Arabis** tied alongside Columbine, and simultaneously they chanted, 'we could pinch one of theirs.

Twenty-eight year old Jack Lavis stood in the port waist as the conspirators came inboard chuckling with anticipated excitement. He too was in a state of excitement for he had just a few days earlier assumed duty as First Lieutenant from Collings who had departed (much to the regret of Turner) on a long course leading to promotion. Turner, on the wing of the Bridge looking aft saw his new Number One as a quiet nice fellow probably capable at his job but obviously inexperienced and a little timid, thinking he might need to chase him awhile to keep him up to things. However subsequent events were to force him to change this opinion.

Chesty and the yeoman went below to find another addition to Mess Six, a signalman by name of Brazier replacing Ordinary Signalman Holland, a move Drewry had decided upon to bring the communications branch to a better standard. But despite the fact that the Londoner could be a possible ally the yeoman and New Zealander decided against letting anyone else into their plot with the exception of Leading Seaman Ken Rousell who had proved his readiness in the past to join other disrespectful undertakings, and they awaited the sailing date of April fifteenth.

It was raining on the 13th and Church Parade was cancelled so the C.O. himself conducted a service on board instead, and as he quoted:

God be in my head and in my understanding.

God be in my eyes and in my looking,

God be in my mouth and in my speaking,

God be in my heart and in my thinking,

God be at mine end and at my departing.

He had little idea of the actions and thoughts the misinterpretation of those lines could invoke in the matelots hunched there in the drizzle. One seaman in particular had just been awarded sixteen days loss of pay for having been adrift sixty hours from special leave to get married. The captain was obliged by King's Regulations to punish him in this manner although reluctant to do so, but the rating having no insight to the true character of his skipper saw something of hypocrisy in those quoted lines; while others were uplifted with the beauty of phraseology and sentiment, and Chesty kicking Drewry's foot muttered, 'I hope the Arabis will be most understanding at our departing.'

Turner could not abide any infringement of the authority invested in his position as commanding officer. He had a fine feeling of sympathy for the rating he had been obliged to punish for overstepping leave. Obliged because K.R's and A.I's (King's Regulations and Admiralty Instructions) were creed and prayer book to him, all other considerations entirely subservient to his conviction that the proper interpretation of these articles were the true mark of a Master. He would tolerate no departure from their strict tenets and therefore demanded and expected complete adherence to his orders. Occasionally it would present awkward confrontation in the days when master and crew were still uncertain of motives and protective of their own abilities, such as the day after the church service when Alfie rang to the Bridge for the Day Log.

Signalman Brazier was duty watch and stood in Alfie's cabin bearing his C.O's curious scrutiny, staring at this unknown rating responding to his summons.

'Who are you?'

'Brazier Sir, replacement to Signalman Holland Sir.'

'I know nothing about this,' said Turner, surprise and a tinge of annoyance in his voice, 'Get the yeoman for me.' Drewry came, giving the Signal Log he carried to Turner without a word, while Brazier sensed the covert hostility between the pair as Turner, also without a word, took the file and read the copy of the signal addressed to Royal Naval Barracks Devonport from Columbine requesting an experienced qualified Signalman.

Turner raised his eyes slowly and said abruptly and testily, 'On whose authority Drewry was this signal made?' Drewry glanced despairingly at Ted Brazier then back to Turner, 'I thought it necessary . . .

'I don't give a hoot what you think Drewry! Interrupted the livid C.O., jabbing a stiffened finger at the file, 'From Columbine? he ground out, 'I am COLUMBINE Drewry and no-one else has the right to usurp that authority!'

Calmly looking into the older man's reddening features and with a maddening exhibition of insubordination leaving Alfie speechless, Drewry replied, 'And I'm in charge of the V/S Department and intend to have the best in the South Atlantic.' Swinging on heel and toe he said to the amazed Ted Brazier, 'C'mon, you get back to the Bridge.'

Though it was not ever proved it is quite possible that the incident provoked the yeoman into proceeding with the plot to steal the Arabis Signal Projector which took place two days later sometime into the Middle Watch, when three men, Ldg Seaman Rousell, Yeoman Drewry, and Trained Operator Wheeler mounted the Bridge under the cover of a moonless night. Rousell clambered on to K.73 to unship the projector as Chesty rigged block and tackle to Columbine's upper yardarm allowing the filched lamp to be raised to that level by the yeoman, then gently lowered out of sight, into the crow's nest where it rested until far into the Atlantic the next day. The consternation of the Arabis signalmen might be surmised, but the jubilant members of Columbine's Bridge were cock-a-hoop with their one-upmanship; no longer forced to stagger from one side of the flag-deck to the other in rough seas, carrying a 'bloody heavy bastard which could easily topple into the bloody 'oggin and send you after it as you attempted to fit it to each alternate support.

Chapter 3

And so they sailed into high and heavy seas with the rollers massive and ponderous peeling over the forecastle and streaming along the waists, weather sufficiently bad to slow down an already slow convoy as one ship after another was compelled to reduce speed. Below in Columbine the mess decks were awash and once again newcomers unused to the peculiar liveliness of corvettes in rough conditions found it imperative to make frequent excursions to the 'Heads', even as Cooks of the Mess encountered definite hazards when conveying food from the galley mid-ships.

Signalman Ted Brazier spent the forenoon on the Bridge then took over the afternoon watch from Chesty so giving him eight hours relief from the unpleasant smell of damp clothing and perspiration permeating all space down below. Hitching himself on the guardrail, holding the handle of the signal projector to retain balance, he began to hum softly to himself in a kind of gravely indeterminate tone 'Life Is Just A Bowl Of Cherries'.

The Navigator, Lt. Trew standing at his desk then situated at the rear of the enclosed inner Bridge, raised an unbelieving eyebrow. He was occupied charting a course brought about by a signal received earlier in the W.T. Office instructing them to detach from the convoy to proceed directly to Gibraltar, and as he heard the sound carried on the wind from the port signal ten inch he wondered if life really could be as simple as expressed so indulgently by the new bunting tosser. He had been minded to marry while the ship had rested in the Tyne, and in fact had done so; but the Admiral had ordered him back the very day after the wedding. Now here he was, with a sentimental signalman, the wide open sea, and going to God knows what, when or where. He strode to the corner of the Bridge to look down, his temper getting the best of him, 'Must you kick up that infernal racket Brazier?' he growled.

The new course and latitude brought calmer seas when the hands were detailed to paint ship and generally clear ravages left by the storm. Everyone now learning more about their jobs and the potential of Columbine as a sea ship, gaining confidence in it and themselves as a consequence. Trew told the captain how he had stood leaning over the Bridge rail the previous night to see a white streak shooting through the dark water straight for the ship too close for anything to be done. He nearly had heart failure he said, practically died on the spot, but nothing happened and further occurrences proved the phosphorescent trails to be porpoise playing round the bows. Alfie smiled at him, 'Now you know what a torpedo will look like - only about ten times as big.'

Gibraltar stood like some giant sphinx gazing across the narrows of the Mediterranean Sea, a prodigious sight to this crew of clerks, costermongers, shop assistants and civil servants. Cox'n Ridley had been there before of course, and Chiefy Bains plus a hand-full of the 'timeservers' but the main body of Columbine personnel sauntering along Main Street jostled by Army swaddies and Air force bods, Spanish workmen and cosmopolitan merchantmen of a dozen nationalities were much taken up with this foreign port where English was the native tongue. Why? Even a British Bobby controlling traffic at the junction of the street leading to The Bristol Bar the fashionable water-hole for officers. Radar Operator Alf McCheyne accompanied by Dennis Alderwick and Bob Mount drank muscatel in a noisy emporium providing this nectar at potent cheapness then ambled into a huge metal shed to squat on wooden stools. This was the Forces Cinema where the ever-popular Goofy and ever-present Donald Duck provided excuse for uninhibited displays of hoots, catcalls and cheers - a welcome release from previous weeks of anxiety and stress.

Threading the dockyard later on their way back to Columbine berthed in the destroyer pens West Mole, McCheyne shot a quizzical glance toward one of his oppos, 'What's the pendant number of Columbine Dennis?'

Alderwick gave an astonished grunt, 'You know bloody well what the number is Alf - 94, it's K.94.

'Yeah, Now add the digits together. What do they come to?'

'Why, thirteen,' replied the mystified chap.

'Right again. Now when was K.94 launched?'

'Thirteenth of August last year . . . hey what're you getting at?'

'And then we collided with the Aberdeen, got off Scot free almost and spent a very nice time laid up' continued McCheyne slowly.

'Well, I don't see what . . . '

'Think about it Dennis,' smiled Alf, quickening his step, 'Yeo gave me the Gen that we're joining the 13th Destroyer Flotilla . . . the thirteenth Dennis, that must mean something eh?'

Well did it mean something? It certainly can be put on record that the thought weighed considerably on the mind of the Radar mechanic in his extra capacity as ship's barber tending to the needs of E.R.A. Stan Parkinson that evening when an irate bellow came from the articifer, 'Watch what you're doing bucko, nearly 'ad me soddin ear then!'

'Bloody sorry Stan, something else on me mind' apologised Dennis and tried to convince himself that he was not superstitious, that the stories of the third match, or of ladders or of the number thirteen were mostly myths.

The Columbine sailed for Freetown the next day enduring slight rough weather though not at all like the stuff thrown at them in the North Atlantic, so by the 2nd May it was calm enough to bring out the dolphins and flying fish to spin and glint in the sun. One fish flew inboard and was picked up by Leading Seaman Prossor who came to the Bridge to show it to the captain, who told him to have it for his breakfast. 'Tastes rather like whiting when cooked properly, lad', advised Alfie.

They were now enjoying really glorious weather, North East Trades with a following wind strong enough to cool things down. The officers were able to lunch on salads that Peppin had obtained and, due to the extra large refrigerator could store. The rationed populace of Britain could not boast of such abundance as cold beef and potatoes with a salad of lettuce, tomato, egg, chopped beetroot and Spanish onion, followed by banana and tangerine with custard, finishing with cheddar cheese, biscuits, and, butter! As far as the occupants of the wardroom were concerned the whole state of the war had developed into a luxury cruise. Once after such a lunch Alfie alerted the ship's company to an anti submarine exercise and during its course, to accustom those of his crew who hadn't seen depth charges dropped with their resultant explosion, dropped two. 'By a co-incidence' he later wrote to Polly, 'We happened to be over a bank and up came a whole lot of beautiful fish! As there was not much sea and as further experience for the crew in boat work, I went back and dropped a boat, when the lads picked up about seventy pounds of fish - lovely fat firm fellows of about four to six pounds each. Rather like salt water bream and enough for two meals for the whole crew.'

Turner was feeling on top of the world at this moment; looking forward to a scrap with the enemy, sure of his ship's company and the spirit of comradeship already burgeoning both in the Lower Deck and in the Ward-room which had just been augmented by his fifth officer, Sub.Lt. Palmer, who stood with him on the Bridge looking down at the men as they scrubbed an awning. The young officer tried to hide a smile as the ratings turned the hose on each other, fearing an outburst from his new skipper, but Alfie swayed gently with the easy motion of his ship content to allow the whooping and dancing. 'Carrying on like school boys' he thought, 'well as long as they do their work they ought to have some fun'

Biggins, Nuttall and Victim - Carrying on like a bunch of school boys

Tuesday the 6th May brought a surge of activity in the wake of feverish instructions from Base. The previous night had seen a sinking so Columbine was bursting ahead at full speed in an endeavour to catch the perpetrator and afterwards possibly pick up survivors if in life-rafts, but didn't expect to reach the position until long after dark. Meantime they pushed forward through a sea full of porpoises, shark, barracuda, and rays as big as dining-tables which leapt clear out of the water, while look-outs skimmed the placid surface for signs far more dangerous. Night fell as it does in those latitudes, quickly, and the following morning the port look-out reported an object requiring investigation.

The raft, for such it was, rocked lonely and desolate upon the open sea containing nothing more than one shoe, a shoe-tree, and a coat hanger. Questions without adequate answer which had neither name buzzed throughout Columbine as the crew gazed on the pathetic and abandoned life support which had no name or clue as to its owner. Why just the one shoe? Did some mad sad soul jump from its safety in a fit of despair? Turner shrugged and gave the helmsman the order to resume the original course, intercepting a merchantman the next morning and going close alongside to talk with her through the loud-hailer. She turned out to be British and bound for Freetown, sailing alone. She had seen nothing. But for the lads in K.94 it felt quite like a link with home out in those calm waters and when the convoy was reached and normal speed resumed, a boom was rigged out with a spinner attached to the end of sounding wire. For a brief moment those conditions denied possibilities that a lurking hidden enemy could, at any time, strike against Columbine or her charges. A fish did bite that evening but so huge must it have been and so fiercely did it bite that the wire was sheared through and the spinner dropped to the bottom of the 'oggin. It was the 8th May; they arrived at Freetown some time into the 'First' watch.

Relieved from Entering Harbour Routine, the Cox'n left the wheelhouse making his way aft to stand with the buffer who was leaning on the port gunwale savouring the hot scented breeze coming off-shore across the smooth black water of the harbour, his eyes fixed on the gently rocking patterns of light reflected from waterfront buildings.

'Bloody 'ell, what a stinking pong!' moaned Glanville, 'Called the White Mans Grave this place aint it? God, it smells like there's millions of rotting carcasses over there.' Muttering savagely Peter Ridley swotted a brace of mosquitoes.

'I'll have to do something about these little buggers. Trouble is Bill' he answered, 'you've not got an educated nose, but I reckon you'll soon get used to it as your ancestors probably did.'

'What the dickens d'you mean Peter?'

'Don't you know? This place was called Glanvilletown once, way back, somewhere around the seventeen hundreds I think.'

'Come off it Peter. Anyway, it wouldn't have been our branch of the family or I wouldn't be buffer of Columbine you can bet your boots.'

The cox'n stretched his arms and yawned, 'Well actually I heard the skipper telling young Palmer about it yesterday. Glanvilletown he said . . .or maybe it was Granville town . . . might not have heard it properly . . . '

'You're full of flannel 'swain; that's why I don't believe that yarn you were spinning in the mess t'other day about getting a medal from the King of Romania. What a loada bull that is!'

'Now that is true, straight up an' cross me heart. He gave me a medal and brevet for Valour and Fidelity when I was at Constanza on the Black Sea sixteen years ago. September 7th it was, 1925 . . . I remember it well.'

'O.K. where is it then, I've never seen you wear it ever.'

'Because its against Naval Regulations to wear foreign decorations that's why.'

Glanville cast a suspicious eye at Peter, 'I'm turning in' he said shortly, 'Goodnight,' leaving the cox'n to wonder why some people found it difficult to take him seriously.

Left alone he paused awhile before following his friend, allowing himself the luxury of unaccustomed drawing aside of curtains to his past which then had seemed so secure and full of promise; especially when compared to the present uncertainties. 'My gosh' he thought to himself, 'nearly half my lifetime ago. Forty I am now and I was only a young lad coming up twenty-five when I got that medal. Mind you' he mused, 'I was a lot older on the old Frobisher than some of these boys I've got on Columbine now.' He took a final look round his small domain and walked to the companion-way grinning as he went, 'I'll tell Bill tomorrow it wasn't the King of Romania who gave me the medal because he'd taken the day off sick, and it was really his queen who made the presentation- - bet he won't believe that either.'

Jack Lavis approached Ridley next day as the hands were engaged in their various forenoon activities to say that he'd much appreciate some help with the ship's correspondence. The problem was quickly solved by typical Naval efficiency. The coxswain awaited 'Stand-easy', then bringing the lads together on the engine-room casing made known the First Lieutenant's dilemma, and explaining . . . 'What is required is a voluntary man,' his eyes finding a seaman preparing to ignite a 'tickler' the rolled tobacco jutting from the ham-fisted cigarette maker's mouth like a witch's broom-stick. 'Yes, you' he beamed, 'You'll do nicely Williams; worked in a Bank before the war I believe so it'll be just the job for your talents. Report to Number One after Stand-easy and tell him I volunteered you to help him.'

When they went off in the Liberty boat that afternoon the ratings discovered Freetown a far different run ashore than Gib. It was dusty, the shacks and grass huts either side of the main thoroughfare were higgledy-piggledy, there was a sort of bazaar flogging trinkets and gaudy baubles with glimpses of unadorned native girls enticing the passing matelot - including Columbine's matelots, some of whom succumbed to their black glances all too readily. Others however walked the tight-rope of abstinence even so far as to eschew the beer ration, making their way instead to nearby Lumley Beach to spend a leisurely afternoon swimming and flirting innocently with the dusky beauties of the sand's edge. It was a great deal hotter too which led to the perspiration creating dhoby-itch on those unaccustomed to launder their clothing with proficiency. Of course they had been warned that they shouldn't indulge too frequently in sun-bathing; most of them respecting this advice, keeping either to the water or the shade, but one young Leading Seaman omitting precaution put everyone in a bit of a panic when, at sea later, he was found in a state of utter exhaustion on the upper deck showing a temperature of 105.6 degrees.

Leading Seaman Peppin fancied himself as a doctor and was all for using ice packs from the refrigerator, a procedure full of hazard thought Jack Lavis, but consensus of opinion waived aside scruple and the fortunate rating did actually recover within a few days so giving time for the Number One to forget his doubts, with a new-found interest - a small monkey he'd brought aboard from the last run ashore.

The ship continued its exertions as 'canteen-boat' of the escort group comprising **Clematis**, Columbine, **Cyclamen, Gardenia** and the sloop **Sandwich** - a sort of general dogs-body to be detailed by the Senior Officer of the group for all manner of inconvenient tasks. Plying the trade routes between Freetown and the Azores chivvying the merchantmen: bawling out stragglers, pleading for less smoke, scurrying back and forth in procedural zig-zag, one day pretty much the same as the last; including perpetual vigilance which had to be kept fresh and awake. The Germans had about a dozen submarines roaming the North Atlantic at the time and in order that they might divert or divide the British forces had deployed several more around the Freetown area where, during the month of May these marauders sent thirty-two merchantmen to Davy Jones'; one being the 'Marissa' whose lifeboat Columbine chanced upon when as 'Gash-Hand', she was detached as usual from the convoy on the 20th May.

She was on the far perimeter of the convoy sailing alone, out of sight, her speed down to about six knots, in touch with the Senior Officer by Admiralty signals, because everyone was afraid of her from the Commodore down to the cook on the slowest tramp, and her own crew were none too happy either.

For some reason the engines just would not 'run in' properly and after a few hours steaming would develop a shattering 'big end' knocking which would frighten the life out of all on board listening to the reverberating rumble being carried on the waves toward listening devices of U-boats. The fault had manifested a few weeks previously but no amount of expertise at Freetown could solve the trouble, and when the ship put to sea a pronounced 'remedy' continuously proved ineffective, the half demented Bains and his team applying oily waste and foul language with impotent regularity and no result. So it became the routine for the S.O. to send the 'canteen boat' as far away as possible or practicable to enable her to assist in any emergency, but it was Bob Bains' conviction that they were being used as a decoy as he lay in his bunk imagining the knock knock knock running through the ocean as a postman's knock on Jerry giving the news that K94 was knocking about in that U-boat infested sea.

The look-outs were doubled up and off-duty men kept a wary eye to sea-ward if they spent any time on deck, and so it came about that Brazier saw the craft as he relaxed on the fo'c's'le sun-bathing. It was off the port bow, relatively near when he spotted it, hopping to his feet to bawl to Signalman McCall on the Bridge. 'See it Keir? Small boat, about Red 05!'

By this time Columbine was already slewing to port, Ted's shout had alerted the O.O.W. who had altered course to close and vet the small whaler which now began to lower a sail, and as they drew nearer Brazier saw that the boat bore the name S. S. **Marisa** and it contained three officers, white men, and nine or ten crewmen who appeared to be Chinese, all seemed to be unhurt except one fellow lacerated about the face. After they had been brought aboard it became apparent that the officers were Dutchmen so arrangements were made to accommodate them aft, while the others were sent forward to the mess decks after the steward had investigated the slight injuries sustained by some of them. A rub of oil or a dab of ointment sufficed in most cases but when it came to the fellow with cuts on his face he asked him what he'd done to himself.

'Plice sir, bloken gauge into face, never mind no wully.'

8029 Ton Dutch tanker 'Marissa' sunk 40 miles S.W. Freetown U-107 Kapitan-Leutnant Gunter Hessler

Cleaning up the face in front of him Peppin murmured an aside to Seaman Eatough who had assisted the survivors aboard, 'You understand the chink Dave?'

Eatough grinned as the pipe came over, 'Pom-Pom guns' crew close up at the double' and moving away to its summons replied, 'Better than I can understand you boyo, he said he was cut by a broken glass gauge and not to worry.' And dashing up to the two-pounder found Leading Seaman McNichol already preparing the weapon for action while to port he saw Torpedo-seaman George Carstairs assisting Sub.Lt Palmer in the process of bringing the whaler's sails on board Columbine for subsequent use as an awning for Alfie.

The propeller began to turn as Columbine stood away, Turner's intention was to sink the boat with gun-fire, the honour lying to the marksmanship of the cock-sure McNichol who, at the given order gleefully began firing, and kept on firing.

Not one hit was registered at all as K.94 reached five knots, and as she began circling the life-boat the accursed big-end dissonance began again. The Dutch officers listened to the racket and looked at one another, then the senior of them moved to Alfie's side plucking at his sleeve and saying, 'Please, our boat is yet undamaged Captain, may we ask you to let us return to it and continue alone our journey to Africa; we have charts, it will be safer I think?'

'Nonsense' snapped Turner, swinging round, 'my ship's perfectly safe, and the guns' crew just a little out of practice, which time and Mr.Lavis will remedy. See to it Number One will you?'

Forty-one rounds of H.E. were expended to sink the boat, the last one, in the studied assessment of the watching Dutchmen, quite superfluous as, on two counts they offered their experience to help Bains in the engine room. He agreed with some reluctance although the rest weren't so certain of any outcome when the ship was stopped while engine-room artificers and stokers got busy in the filthy grease and oil, a labour of hit and miss, biffs and thuds with spanners and hammers thunderously echoing miles under the water as every soul thought, but couldn't voice the possibility of torpedoes.

Every available man placed on lookout duty for signs of an attack by U-boat, and those not so employed finding excuse to remain on the upper deck. Any attempt of mine to illustrate the passing of those year-long hours would be completely inadequate. We have read of similar accounts, watched the facsimile event in film at the cinema, which I'm fairly certain Monsarrat heard while gleaning material for his book in the Naval Canteen at Gladstone Dock Liverpool, but The Senior Service lives up to its reputation and all those in terror for the smallest sign of the stronger enemy at that time are reluctant to exhibit those feelings again.

At last capitulating to the gremlin the Chief E.R.A. and the Dutch helpers came to the Bridge to report failure to Turner.

'Can I move my ship Chief?' asked Alfie.

'Yes, Captain, but slowly - as before,' replied Bains morosely, leaving the Bridge conscious of frustration alien to his native resolution and finding the irritation mounting within himself when he stood in the engine room observing the peculiar behaviour of Petty Officer Stoker, Murphy who was putting a hand on the throttle wheel then lowering his head to give the impression that he was listening to something. He would then appear to speak, although Bob could hear nothing above the noise of the crankshaft, repeating this manoeuvre, each occasion with decreasing concern on his face. Bob fought down nerves as they twitched and bunched. 'What the blue blazes d'you think you're at Spud! he bawled, 'off your trolley are you?'

Murphy sprung round at the uncharitable irascibility, surprised and hurt at this unusual side of his chief, 'Come over here chief, and listen.' He then patted the wheel and this time Bob heard him mutter, 'You can do it.' then glance sideways at the C.E.R.A. to say, 'Hear that? It's saying I can do it, I can do it, I can do it, I can do it.'

'Thundering Moses, I believe you' ejaculated Bob as the thought percolated through pent up fibres at the incongruity of a grown man attaching such immense reliance in a stupid machine but it eased his sleep, even though his cynicism made him alive to the conviction that the trouble wouldn't vanish with the wish and sure enough, when aroused the next morning it was to the accompaniment to those same nerve-wracking blows as the ship kept to her slow regulated passage to Freetown.

However nothing untoward took place and shortly after reaching port Percy Drewry enthusiastically persuaded Ted Brazier to take advantage of the pipe 'Hands to bathe'. The communications branch were all competent swimmers and usually enjoyed the relaxation whenever possible. However, after ten minutes or so Ted felt a sting below his left ankle, climbing back inboard to sit watching the foot gradually suffuse and swell. This alarmed Drury no end and off he went to fetch Peppin who eyed the inflammation diagnosing it of no great consequence but, 'I'll get you sent over to the hospital on the Edinburgh Castle for safety's sake' he said, 'they'll most likely give you some sort of treatment though personally I don't think it's very dangerous.' But Percy swore, 'Sod that for a skylark, I'll not go swimming in these seas again unless I'm damn sure there's nothing in there to bite <u>me</u>!'

Signalman Keir McCall was a professional swimmer and diver, but more at home in a pool, the New Zealander Wheeler however really was a top grade exponent of the sport having several times completed the annual event in Auckland Harbour - indeed he was almost amphibian, so he had no qualms when on the 24th May he stood swaying on the pier waiting very impatiently for the liberty boat. Brazier was duty signalman on the Bridge; Number One on his way aft when they both caught sight of Wheeler hurling himself into the sea quite half a mile from the ship. As he neared Columbine, the Officer of the Watch, Lt.Maguire, ordered him to come on board immediately as Chesty began to flaunt his ability to circle the vessel time and again, ignoring all the implications of impending KR & AI charges, merely yelling at the top of his voice,' It's not dan...gar...us, it aint dan...gar...us!' in the customary mispronounced manner that had endeared him to his shipmates. He stubbornly refused to come aboard under these threats of punishment and despite the strong running current kept up the self-imposed feat of endurance.

'Stupid bastard, he's only making things worse for himself,' Brazier muttered to Drewry who, by this time had joined him on the Bridge to watch the fun as the rest of the ship's company gathered and shouted encouragement or warning to the now flagging Wheeler. And he, having grown tired of his prank came aboard to be awarded 10 A's - not that the imposed extra seaman duties worried him at all as most aspects of this nature came as second nature to a RNZVR yachtsman. Shortly after this episode, the day after actually, the Cox'n and Buffer were chatting on the upper deck by the funnel looking down at the mustering liberty men waiting for the OOD to inspect them. 'You know that Kiwi bunts in the 'rattle' Bill?' asked Ridley, 'did you <u>hear</u> what he was calling out yesterday? Dan gar us. Must be Maori I reckon, can't be English. Just then as Sub.Lt. Palmer released the ratings from scrutiny Peter leaned over the rail. 'Listen lads, because we're sailing tomorrow Lt Palmer here has given out extra beer tickets for you and I want you all to appreciate how extremely *magnamacious* of him it is.' His speech was rewarded with a cheer.

When they returned from this run ashore many of the liberty men had emulated Jack Lavis in bringing back various pets, as <u>he</u> had done on the previous occasion. There was a cock, a hen, and a baby chicken, a mongoose - there might even had been a baby leopard in the complement if Alfie Turner had been able to buy it for one pound instead of the three demanded of him. 'Still,' as he reflected in a letter to Polly, 'it might have proved a problem as it grew up.' The monkey belonging to the First Lieutenant was now a firm favourite with the crew indeed with the captain too who would feed it with milk and other delicacies from the ward-room pantry as he sat beneath the awning on the boat deck enchanted with the sight of the quaint little creature nursing the baby chick and stroking it, a delightful picture. Tragedy struck on the morning of the 28th May when, possibly due to malevolent jealousy the chick was eaten by the mongoose, leaving as evidence of the dastardly crime but a few downy feathers and the small monkey scratching its head and crying over them piteously.

It was glorious weather, a low easy swell under a blue sky, a few cumulous building far to the north when a commotion was observed within the rank and file of the convoy as the Azores came into view. Hands to Dinner had been piped and Ted Brazier stood in the Afternoon Watch rasping aloud another of his inimitable renderings in the jazz idiom as water spouts erupted between the ongoing lines of merchantmen. He stopped on an up-beat and reported the phenomenon to the OOW and Sub.Lt. Palmer immediately leant to the voice-pipe:

'Captain Sir! Convoy is under attack; we can see columns of water rising between ships. Think it could be aerial Sir.'

'Right' came Turner's voice,' Sound action stations and close up anti-aircraft gun crew!' Climbing the ladder he found the augmented Bridge personnel scouring the skies with binoculars sweeping in sections port and starboard, fore and aft.

'Answer the Clematis, signalman!' he shouted as Brazier simultaneously kicked on the power to the port lamp, directing the beam toward the flashing call-sign: - K94 . . . K94 . . .K94 . . . 'To Clematis repeated Columbine' he read, 'From Senior Officer. Believe German heavy unit beyond horizon shelling convoy. Detach and investigate.'

As Lt. McLeod Cleeves swung **Clematis** round to bear off at 17 knots an X48 came winking from her Bridge, a private signal from the Watch to the Watch, Yeoman to Yeoman, P.O. Wynne to P.O. Drewry.

It's purport? 'Mac ordered . . .On tin hats, we do or die lads.'

O/Sig. Keir McCall, Sig. 'Chesty' Wheeler, Sig. Ted Brazier

Leading Steward Albert Baker

'Icky' Thomas

A. B. Bailey, Hateley, C. Davies

However toward evening **Clematis** returned on station. Unlike her earlier encounter with the German cruiser **Admiral Hipper** she had encountered nothing, seen nothing, the enemy evidently possessing superior speed, but the question was, why run from a corvette? It was only the passing weeks that gave news about the destruction of the German battlewagon Bismarck and of the action, which had allowed the **Prinz Eugen** to escape to the south and pursue its offensive against merchantmen. It was many years before it became known that Captain Brinkmann had oiled from the **Esso Hamburg** on the 28th May, and found defective engines and a chipped propeller-blade. Most likely it was a parting salvo loosed against Columbine's charges by the Prinz Eugen before shaping course for Brest. With the British Battle Fleet searching for her she would press on as fast as possible and she arrived there on the 1st June.

The Second Dog-Watch brought news of more gravity when the horrified crew heard the latest bulletin on the devastating battle in the Mediterranean. They sat in silence in the mess decks, each caught up in their own thoughts after the initial outburst of disbelief as the B.B.C. spoke of the loss of two cruisers and four destroyers off Crete. In his cabin Turner began his accustomed daily report to his wife. 'Darling, we are not without our alarms and excursions where we are' he wrote, 'But Polly, this war is truly on a far wider front than the last one was, and I fear we have a long hard furrow to hoe ahead of us.'

The day wore on as the escorts pushed the convoy northwards to the rendezvous where the Group from Gibraltar would take over for the next stage of the journey to the North Channel thus allowing Columbine and her sister ships to return to Base. During the 'First Watch' when darkness spread over quiet waters, Chesty Wheeler leaned across the guard-rail to spit for luck into the sea. Over on the 'Monkey Island' was the Officer of the Watch, Ed Maguire, a Canadian; and here he was, Signalman of the Watch, the officer's right hand man in a way, a New Zealander, and below them, a British ship, with British lives aboard. At about 2300hrs a sudden dim flashing ahead told him that they were in contact with the Gibraltar Group and that he could expect some manoeuvring. Then with a blast of fear he saw a three light signal being exhibited on the ship conveying the Commodore and the ships all around were turning independently, scattering! This could only mean some frantic emergency; a U-boat, or another surface raider - perhaps the Heavy German Unit chased by Clematis had come back to pound the convoy and escorts to Kingdom Come! Perhaps it had brought support. His vivid imagination awaited cataclysm yet over on the Bridge Maguire seemed singularly unperturbed as the darkness swallowed up an ocean of ships For a split second he thought Columbine had responded to an order by Maguire and turned on her zig-zag thus losing sight of the convoy, but plagued still by the incidence of the three light signal he hurriedly sought guidance from the Convoy Instructions and the Consigs Volume as midnight arrived on stockinged feet when the Watch changed.

Ted Brazier tapped his shoulder, making him flinch, 'Good you're here. Blasted convoy seems to have vanished. Just before they went I saw a signal light on the Commodore and I'm buggered if I knew what it meant. I was looking it up in here but can't find it. Here, you might have better luck. Goodnight.'

Ted thumbed through the volume trying to keep a sort of look-out at the same time, over-hearing the enquiring voice of Jack Lavis as he took over from a sleepy Ed Maguire, catching the tail end of the reply from Ed as he vanished below, 'God knows, but it's all yours now, good night.'

Jack angrily called down to him, 'But look here . . .you can't leave me like this . . . not without explanation!' However the Canadian could and did, leaving the new occupants of the Bridge to gaze in bewilderment at one another.

'LOOK OUT!' Brazier screamed, and the First Lieutenant blew an order to the helmsman as the fearsome bows of a destroyer leapt out of blackness on a collision course. Moments later he was signalling with a blue lamp steadying the beat of his heart with the regulated pulse of the Morse Code; ascertaining that the warship was H.M.S. Witch, was one of the relieving Group, and who was also, lost; due to the inexplicable and precipitous dispersal of the convoy. Quickly Ted asked the destroyer's yeoman the meaning of the Commodore's signal and was amazed to be told it had been transmitted by the S.O. of the relieving force from the new book MERSIGS to the Commodore for instruction to the ships under his command but which had quite obviously been misinterpreted. Brazier spoke to Lavis about this, 'Do you have any knowledge of MERSIGS, Sir?'

'No signalman, you'd best ask the yeoman in the morning. Meanwhile the job in hand is to find the S.O. and straighten out this mess.' The mess was finally straightened out though it took the best part of the 'Middle'.

On the port side of the Bridge slightly abaft the Hotchkiss and a foot or so from the signal lamp was a most curious, almost futuristic appendage resembling something from the pen of cartoonist Humphrey Searle. Erected one day in Freetown it was basically a steel platform raised six feet above the deck and upon which rested a mechanical semaphore and a Kleig Searchlight. This searchlight was Brazier's designated 'Action Station'. Cold, unprotected, vulnerable, perched miles above anyone else on the Bridge, the first object he thought, for any surface enemy to use as target practice, and felt intense hatred for the unknown boffin who had dreamt up the Fred Karno idea but as the 'Middle' dragged on toward three and the light wind rustled down a few drops of rain he took advantage of the platform's cover, waiting in solitary watchfulness until relieved by McCall.

Returning from the Azores a week later Chiefy Bains mounted the Bridge to inform the captain that previous manoeuvres had somewhat depleted fuel supplies, producing an expletive from Alfie and a request to the S.O. that Columbine proceed to the Gambia to replenish these stores.

Permission granted Columbine reached Bathurst toward late afternoon or evening on the 9th June. The approaches are notoriously difficult and needed extreme caution to be exercised to navigate the channel in the growing darkness. Darkness that however still allowed yeoman Drury to shudder at a dead shark floating on the surface of light green water at the entrance. A strong and enthusiastic swimmer he might be but the sight put him right off any intention to indulge his passion for the sport. Nearing Government House, a burst of activity alerted Brazier's attention at the Ensign aft when to his astonishment he saw a small party of black soldiers 'Tumble outa their wee hoose at the double'. He afterwards told me, 'Even I felt lordly - and Turner definitely assumed the honorary rank of Admiral as one soldier stood by the flagpole, and the others mustered round an ancient cannon on the forecourt'. At the moment we were directly abreast the Union Flag dipped, the Captain of the Gun saluted, and the cannon roared in a one-gun salute. I dipped our ensign in reply.'

Finding her anchorage it was found that Columbine was the only warship in the place, giving Lavis visions, especially presumptive on their honorific arrival of performing duties more suitable to a cruiser such as the Berwick than the vessel he'd lately come to think of as Alfie's personal yacht. For the captain had certainly shown a love of comfort since they had become acquainted; the deck chairs and early-morning tea, the massive 'fridge acquired to hold a wide variety of salad foods, the inclination toward fresh fish at every opportunity.

Back on the Bridge, Brazier took a signal from Government House proposing that the captain call on the Governor. So the following afternoon the out-board motor was fitted to the cutter and Turner carried across in response to this invitation by Sir Thomas and Lady Sothern. He found a small party in progress, an Air Commodore, a Wing Commander, one or two 'others', and a drink in his hand, when in walked a couple of fellows clad in shorts and open-necked shirts, one of whom looked strangely familiar. The other was a complete stranger.

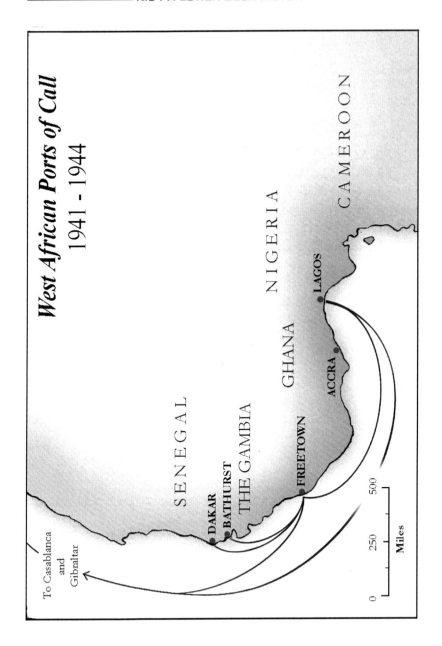

West African Ports of Call
1941 - 1944

Lady Sothern caught Alfie's arm to guide him across to where the new-comers stood by an open window, and pointing out toward Columbine said, 'This is the commanding officer of that warship out there,' introducing him to Captain Lord Louis Mountbatton, a cousin of the King, and to Captain James Roosevelt, eldest son of the President of the United States of America.

Alfie was staggered for the moment but soon regaining composure under the very friendliness of the pair as Lord Louis explained that after the attack on the destroyer **Kelly** under his command off the west coast of Crete, when it and the **Kashmir** were sunk by a formation of twenty four dive-bombers, the destroyer **Kipling** was able to rescue from the sea 279 officers and men, including himself.

'Ah,' said Alfie, 'we heard the news about the disaster out there Sir, the loss of two cruisers and four destroyers. Didn't know Sir,' you were involved in it. . .'

'**Gloucester, Fiji,** and the **Greyhound, Juno, Kashmir**, and my **Kelly**' replied Mountbatton tersely. 'I was picked up and taken to Alexandria then to Cairo. Met this fellow there.'

Roosevelt smiled, 'Have to hitch my way to Lisbon Portugal, then get back to the States. Lord Louis reckons on coming with me and we've decided on tomorrow. Not much food here y'know . . . nor drink.' he added.

Eyes quizzical, Alfie looked about at the laden tables, and his companions grinned like a couple of conspirators, 'Pigeons. Not ours. You see we're staying in Government House and we took a couple of shotguns yesterday to bag six or seven of 'em off the roof. We each fired a shot to make 'em fly in the air then the other brought them down. We made a present of them to our hostess. Hope you like pigeon.'

A short while after the meal Lady Sothern said to Turner, 'Yes, it's quite true, it's becoming rather difficult to obtain proper supplies recently and as a matter of fact my butler whispered to me just before luncheon that we are down to our last dozen bottles of sherry.'

'My goodness,' responded Alfie, 'Well I think we are pretty well stocked on board, may I offer you a case of ward-room sherry?'

'My dear man, of course you may. Oh, you have saved our lives!' she exclaimed rapturously, 'Now you must come and see us again when next you visit the Gambia . . .and, yes, let me see . . .yes, please tell the officers under your command that they can use the Government House tennis courts whenever they choose.'

After this Turner repaired on board, sending the promised case of wine over in the launch, which had brought him back to his ship. He was cock-a-hoop over his excursion with the nobility; the good life was very much to his inclinations, so he grabbed the advantage he had apparently secured with Lady Sothern to despatch an invitation to dinner onboard Columbine before she left the Gambia, then instructed the crew to have the ship ready in all respects for inspection by the august pair. This was not looked upon with much favour by the matelots steaming in the foc'sle mess-decks, in harbour, without the alleviating comfort of a sea breeze. Lower deck conversation broadened as careless of feedback someone was heard to complain, 'It aint bleedin' right Buffer, 'avin the bloody ship tarted up in this wever and women shouldn't come on warships anyhow.'

'You just get on with it lad' admonished Glanville sympathetically, 'I'll break out the limejuice at Stand-easy. Remember you're only doing what all sailors have to do in warships - as the captain bloody well tells them.'

The awning was adjusted on the quarterdeck starboard side below the rear of the Bridge; the table laid with submissive care by P.O. Steward Peppin who was to attend to the guests' epicurean requirements, then man the gramophone. Columbine proved indeed to have a finer cellar than Government House as wine and spirit flowed copiously through the veins of Sir Thomas and his lady wife while Alfie expansively drew upon a store of anecdote. The party chuckled then roared its way toward the dark hours until the proprieties called a halt, and the punctilious knight departed with an enlightened lady who now knew the truth contained in the song . . . well you know what sailors are, bright and breezy, free and easy. Etc. etc.

On receipt of sailing orders - which came all too soon, Turner navigated the narrow channel to pass the Sothern residence, as he did so he caused the loud-hailer to be rigged facing the house and called,' Hello, hello. Thanks for hospitality,' when the ships company were rewarded with the sight of fluttering handkerchiefs. It is on record however that the ship never returned to the Gambia, the officers never got to play love all at the courts tennis or otherwise, and the ratings weren't altogether taken up with their 'limers'. So they steamed south again, to Freetown, the banging engine (P.O. Ted Witts used a rather more picturesque adjective) giving a repetition of those fears which had been arrested during their time in port. Apprehensive, jittery, 'Doc' Rowlands and his telegraphists kept attentive watch on Admiralty signals; in his off-duty periods Malcolm Salisbury continued his experiments to detect a system of radio detecting beams that would put Columbine in the fore-front of any corvette at that time not so equipped. Then the bloody rudder jammed. Suddenly; on a zig, or maybe it was a zag, Lt. Trew was then on watch talking with the 'bunts.' He broke off to order the helmsman, 'Port ten.'

'Ten degrees of port wheel on Sir' came the immediate response.

'Steer one eight oh.'

'Course one eight oh Sir.'

Just seconds later Trew threw himself at the pipe snapping, 'Watch your heading man. Who is that on the wheel?'

A panicky voice floated up, 'Able Seaman Stanley, Sir, there's something wrong Sir, she won't steer!'

'You'd better send someone to fetch the cox'n pronto and tell the Chief E.R.A. to report to the Bridge. Make it lively.'

Then, with a perversity characteristic with Columbine's relationship with the sea the situation righted before the messenger moved from the wheelhouse.

'Bridge!'

'Yes, what is it?'

'She's working again Sir, I can feel her O.K. we're steady on course one eight oh, Sir.'

Trew heaved a sigh of relief, shooting a glance toward McCall but saying nothing, only too happy that he would have no need to call the captain to the Bridge - yet. To Stanley he called, 'Very good. Keep her steady. In a few moments we shall alter course again - keep on your toes. Is she still behaving?'

'Yessir.'

'Very good.'

The first 'dog' closed without further incident, discounting the minor defect to their magnificent refrigerator.

Prior to his relief, Trew noticed Baker and Peppin bringing food to the waists putting it there obviously until nightfall when it could be dumped over the side, so when Maguire came up he asked, 'What's going on with those provisions down there? Have they gone off, Ed?'

'Darn 'fridge, how d'you say? Gone for a Burton? Yeh, Tanky can't fix it no-how but says we've got plenty of bully beef on board. Didn't seem too bothered when he came to the wardroom to report it but Turner's like a bull with a sore head. I'd watch it when you get down there if I were you . . . he tore a strip off me because I humorously offered to buy a Yankee model when we hit port. Take care, chum.'

'W/T Office . . . Bridge, received a dis . . . ' The rest of the shout became indistinct as Maguire accompanied Trew to the four steps leading off the 'Monkey Island' then returned to the voice-pipe.'

'Repeat that, will you W/T.'

'Yes Sir.' and Salisbury repeated, 'We've received a distress call from a Norwegian tanker southwest from Freetown,' and he went on to give bearings. Turner was alerted to the situation and ordered a change of course to bring them to the position radioed by the stricken vessel. However by the time Columbine reached there it had gone down leaving one small boat filled with men whose exhausted bodies were covered in oil. Three or four of them had swallowed some; one of them died in hospital on reaching Freetown.

This time the K94 liberty men made for King Tong, spending their rations then resorting to Palm wine. The liberty boat, when it drew alongside that night contained a heap of as near incapable matelots as anyone is ever likely to encounter. Arms, legs heads entwined, uniforms in disarray, slurred incomprehensible talk undignified by the term 'speech'; and a line of 'Captain's Defaulters' as would stretch from stem to stern thought the First Lieutenant. Hurriedly giving orders for them to be hauled inboard before going below to appraise the skipper of the situation, recommending that Turner keep to his cabin. 'What the eye doesn't see, Sir . . .' he persuaded. Providentially, the famous Lavis diplomacy bore fruit on this occasion, and the hands never quite repeated the debacle in such numbers again although there were many instances in the future when one or another was put 'in the rattle' for imbibing the juice of the palm to such incontinence that the King's uniform was, in the eyes of Alfred Lawrence Turner, thoroughly disgraced and the King's Regulations in this regard, heartily enforced.

Chapter 4

Alfie Turner left the ship on the 9th August, coming that day from F.O.I.C. Freetown to tell Steward Albert Baker that he required his bags and trunk to be carefully packed and made available for the afternoon. He then made his way to the Wardroom where he informed Lavis of his impending departure.

The 'buzz' ravelled the ship like the proverbial 'dose of salts' and speculations on reasons and causes for Alfie's going were wild, nefarious, or hopeful depending upon the predilection of the individuals concerned. Subby Palmer burst into the Wardroom, amazement in his eyes. 'I say Number One, I just heard Ridley telling what's-is-name - the Buffer, that the Old Man's been made a knight and he's going to take over the Gambia!' He stood in the doorway, the excitement dripping away as he saw smiles appearing on the faces of his fellow officers. 'Not true,huh? He is leaving though isn't he?'

'Yes, he's going; actually he's taking off this afternoon to K.17, the Amaranthus,' Lavis responded flatly, 'He's to put matters right in her he says.' There was a pause which some writers put down as being pregnant then Bagsy Baker put his head under the subby's arm saying to Lavis: 'Excuse me Sir, skipper's gear ready Sir.' Thank you Baker, I'll let him know,' acknowledged Jack absently, his mind on the future.

However - three days later Turner returned, writing to Polly,' I am back on my own dear ship . . . I was re-appointed and came back rejoicing! And back all my baggage came. Poor Baker had a rotten time, packing everything up carefully and unpacking again in three days . . .'

The time spent on the corvette **Amaranthus** had convinced him that it was not at all like Columbine, and when a lightening tour had persuaded him that the reported defects were ill founded he called at Base H.Q. asking that he be given back his old command. Freetown had insufficient skills to right the K.94 rudder troubles at that time, which meant a twelve hundred mile journey to dry dock, a voyage rather tricky and under circumstances when anyone experienced enough was loath to take it on, those willing to try, not sufficiently qualified; Alfie's request was granted. Thus on the 13th August - yes, another thirteen, Columbine hoisted the flags 'INT Item Jig' requesting permission to leave port, turning south amid torrential squalls, which blotted vision and made the swept channel an area of terror as the ship broke down six times in an hour. The continuously jamming rudder expended the limited vocabulary of the suffering crew jumping to the versatile orders of the one real sailor on board as he manipulated his 'dear ship' with finesse and resourcefulness. When she eventually stood clear out to sea ploughing along, steered by hand from the Steering Flat aft, helm orders needed to be bellowed down a speaking tube from the Bridge. It was a test of endeavour, a time of effort, and the entire crew pulled together; each at his separate station, each as part of a team, striving to one end.

Four days out attention was focused on a lone ship on the horizon. The silhouette was uncertain and unrecognisable. With the troublesome rudder having partial remedy, or being seemingly contained, Turner opted to give chase, having the suspicion that the intruder could be an enemy supply vessel - especially as the flashing signal projector could awaken not the slightest glimmer from the ship steering a parallel course to him. However the incident proved negative - much to Alfie's disappointment for he was longing for his hour of glory - the uncommunicative merchantman turned out to be a foreigner certainly, but a neutral, a Portuguese. The day in fact was one of alarums when action stations was twice piped before the 'second dog' when low-lying land poorly charted, was observed to Port. Perhaps overcautiously keeping to sea-ward, Columbine found herself mixed up in a north-bound convoy in the pitch-black night with such imminent risk that Turner felt that he could trust no-one but himself with the responsibility, so remained on the Bridge until day-break; over-riding the First Lieutenant's insistence that <u>he</u> could manage very well.

There was a curious dictatorial failing in Alfie. Unquestionably a very fine sailor, as a commanding officer he was disposed to pontificate, decisions were irrefutable and rarely modified. He still saw Lavis as 'a quiet fellow and obviously rather inexperienced' in spite of the months at sea when Jack had shown his ability time and again. This was proven further when Jack's papers caught up affirming that on joining his previous ship, the Pomeral, as Navigating Officer, Commander Tyminsky, the C.O. asked for him as his First Lieutenant when the then 'Jimmie' left due to illness. A Free French vessel with a Polish captain and Jack as second in command could scarcely be rated as 'inexperience'. This was Alfie's Achilles Heel, unable to change a snap assessment; he was right, he <u>had to be</u>, the life of the ship, his command, depended on it. Obdurate in this belief, he kept his self-imposed vigil from the swift invasion of the West African night through to the equally speedy rise of the sun. The signalmen and look-outs keyed to expectancy as the procession of vague shapes tossed to port and starboard, horrible in their bulky menace and although the captain was on the Bridge, few of the crew felt the solace of sleep - the cox'n particularly; on 'top line' for a strident call to take him on the wheel.

Just after seven bells in the morning watch they were clear; Alfie set course for Lagos then went to his cabin sleeping until eleven thirty when the vitality or delight maybe, of Able seaman King hammering seven blows on the ship's bell brought him from slumber a trifle bemused and suffering a twinge of heartburn. Summoning Lavis to his cabin he recommended that the ratings be given a 'Make and Mend' period that afternoon; he then took a bath, shaved, enjoyed a salad lunch, and while the crew busied themselves dhobying, darning, writing or playing cards, he spent a quiet afternoon sitting in his deck chair in idle reminiscence. Thinking of the ports and anchorages he had seen and visited before the war, it crossed his mind that he was to enter a strange harbour on the morrow, one he'd never been to before. The chart indicated a narrow channel and as he meditated on the inconstancy of the rudder he began to foresee all kinds of dangers. Out of the corner of his eye he caught sight of Ldg Seaman Prosser moving aft with a hammock casing rolled up under his arm, and beckoned him over, 'Ask the messenger to get a signal pad and bring it here will you lad.' The signal pad was brought and he drafted the following to the authorities at Lagos: - 'Due to uncertain rudder movements request assistance of tug to enter port. My E.T.A. 0900 tomorrow.' Giving the pad to the waiting seaman, telling him to take it to the wireless office for immediate transmission, he felt much better settling further into his chair and calling for Baker.

They made port as anticipated, the 19th August, and preparations put in hand right away to rectify the engine and steerage faults that had bedevilled Columbine for months. Alfie managed to persuade the local padre to come aboard that first Sunday, with the expectation that a proper parson in cassock and surplice would provide a pleasant welcome change for the ship's company, and give authorised Christian guidance to those souls normally falling within his compass.

The island of Lagos has an area of some four square miles - maybe a little smaller - with the town and docks situated toward the western tip; populated by natives, policed and governed and controlled by a small British contingent. The chaplain addressed himself to the task of safe-guarding the well-being of this fresh cohort of Jack Tars, pleading for their enlightenment, warning them of possible consequences etc, and as he gazed upon the youthful faces mustered in front of the make-shift altar he was satisfied with the work he was doing and promised Alfie that he would come again the following Sunday trusting the men had profited by listening to the 'word of God'. Sadly, as is the way of all flesh, some of his well meaning utterances fell on stony ground. In mitigation it needs be realised the entire crew and certainly the stokers, had endured days of unremitting toil - danger even - and were now bent on relief in the only way most natural to them. The various branches of the Lower Deck were now, after such close proximity, consorting amicably. A shared bath-room is a great leveller, and although Alfie Turner went to the open-air cinema to see a Gracie Fields movie that he didn't enjoy overmuch, Signalman Brazier, Seaman Taff Edwards, Coder 'Icky' Thomas, Gunnery rating Tommy Carr, and Seaman Jock Bruce found the friendship of a Nigerian princess and her consort, getting a photograph as memento of the occasion . . .Unfortunately, after they had failed to induce Stoker Les Harding to stay with them, off he went with plans of his own, and with him, two oppoes from the Boiler Room, to reconnoitre . . . nay I must be truthful . . .to imbibe the local brew; and the liquor being as it was, and the temperature inciting magnificent thirst, it wasn't very long before they had exhausted their pay and were making their own convoying zig-zag across the island. The sight of a gleaming Rolls Royce parked in the forecourt of an imposing building incited this émigré from Oxfordshire with notions of one day owning a Morris Cowley, to pull his companions over to investigate the unattended vehicle.

'What's the flag for?' questioned one examiner, pointing to the small banner on the bonnet, 'D'you s'pose it's the <u>King's</u> car?'

'Don't be so stupid, yer great poop! expostulated Les, 'There's no king of Lagos, they only 'ave chiefs, an' so it would be flying a bunch of feathers wouldn't it? Anyway, can anybody drive one of these things?

No one knew afterwards how it actually came about, but the limousine drew away with the three stokers seated abaft the fluttering pennant, none of whom were able to arbitrate on who was to drive or who to navigate, but somehow the amazing Columbine lucky anchor provided its usual protection enabling the trio to reach the jetty without mishap. It was their bad luck, however, to have been observed and enquiries set afoot by the owner rapidly produced results when he had his secretary draw up a letter to the Commanding Officer of H.M.S. Columbine inscribed thus: His Lordship the Viceroy, deprecates the action of three sailors from the ship now enjoying the hospitality of Lagos, but, would press no charges; indeed, would encourage the Commanding Officer to be lenient insofar to the boundaries of discipline.

It is a pleasure to relate that the period of 'jankers' was more of an inconvenience than a trial for the three 'skates.'

Indeed, life settling to routine without the excitement of war became rather slack due to the enforced idleness and a growing conviction that the engine troubles would never be righted, that they were doomed to sweat it out for the duration - physically as well as literally. The Wardroom had things a little easier. There was a club ashore frequented by the business fraternity - Europeans of course - to which they were invited, and nearby, a tolerable golf links enabling Alfie to match points with bank managers, those ubiquitous participants of the sport, and their customers following the ball with the hope of a loan. Many of these indulged a bachelor type of existence in fine houses supported by colonies of servants, their wives having been stranded or sent home to England prior to the war. It is probable many of them had read Somerset Maugham. The young Canadian Maguire and Sub.Lt Palmer received an invitation to meet the young ladies at a party given by one of these generous Englishmen. A famous dish called 'Ground-nut Stew provided sustenance consisting, chicken, rice, hard-boiled eggs, with various vegetables and fruits mixed together with a ground-nut sauce. Another delicacy was entitled, 'Palm Oil Chop'.

Alfie resumed his cinema visits with '*Batchelor Mother*', a David Niven and Ginger Rogers frolic which pleased him more than the Gracie Fields second feature, and he also made friends with a certain Harry Dunn who insisted that Alfie should take on to Columbine a gilded cage holding two parakeets. Really, the ship was fast getting to look like a menagerie, creatures of all kinds and sizes were being carried over the gangway by officers and ratings alike, until the final and most repulsive of the lot was enlisted on the 4th September 1941, contributing to the event now about to be related.

The 5th September came to be known as, 'The Day of the Fiery Dance.' It began as did most days in that overheated period when both officers and men sweated in dry-dock plagued by insects. The living quarters aboard were battlefields of carnage as flying beetles and flies bombarded and swooped like Kamikaze pilots impervious to the swipes and swats splattering them against the bulkheads by the squadron. Yeoman Drewry was getting more and more irritated by conditions in the 'Chiefs and P.O's Mess' and had at last hit upon 'the final solution.' An ingenious method on how he could decimate the hordes while employing the least effort.

The last evening ashore had seen him in the course of barter with a native and coming from negotiation, clutching a canvas bag tied at the neck by a loop of leather imprisoning something within that jerked suggesting it might be a bird or a tiny animal.

'What have you got there, Percy?' asked P.O. Witts cautiously eying up the bag.

'Never you mind Ted, just wait till tomorrow. It's a sort of surprise for 'Peter the Meticulous'

But a different sort of surprise awaited Ridley, one that had been fermenting the past couple of months in a large cooking utensil secreted within the darkness of a steel locker. It was a most potent; some would aver pernicious, concoction known as 'The Witches Brew'. Twenty-four eggs in their shells had been deposited together with the juice of twenty-four lemons and left. When inspection established that the shells had dissolved, one bottle of whisky, one bottle of gin, one bottle of proof rum, and half a bottle of sherry was stirred into the mixture with chants plus selected benevolent cuss-words and left to work up steam for a completely random number of weeks.

It had been decided by a quorum that September the Fifth would be most auspicious for this particular beverage to have its secrets revealed.

The cox'n almost dropped his knife and fork on to the mess table as he stared in horror beyond the Chief E.R.A, his voice gurgling in disbelief as he attempted to assume nonchalance, ' Er, Percy, . . . do you know you've got a bloody animal on your plate?'

He was looking at a weird triangular-headed creature cautiously circumnavigating the P. O. Tel's plate. He felt unable to take his eyes off the repulsive face and found himself as hypnotised and helpless as the unfortunate flies settling on the lip of the plate before getting scooped up by a protrusive and tubular tongue.

'What is it, it's horrible, it's making me feel sick. Get it off!'

Amid laughter Percy could be heard protesting that his pet was quite harmless, it was in fact, a baby chameleon and that he had engaged it as his personal fly-catcher. 'There he goes. . . see . . . he doesn't touch the grub on me plate at all, he's very careful.'

'I don't give a toss!' almost shrieked Peter,' It's ugly, it's damn indecent, it's really making me ill just to look at it. Do get rid of it there's a good chap.'

Percy laughed, 'O.K. Peter, if you're that squeamish, but he'll be on duty when you aren't here.' adding 'Happy birthday cox'n.'.

'How did you know that?' Peter gasped, but by then his messmates were into the usual salutation, shaking him by the hand to congratulate him on his forty-first birthday whilst cups or mugs were brought to drink his health. And to drink his health, and again, to drink his health, for, after the initial imbibing of the Witches Brew one connoisseur pronounced a lack of sugar, with the second libation some other graduate of cordon bleu remarked that the colour missed out a trifle, and after the third emptying of mugs and cups, a proposal was raised that the birthday lad shifted into his birthday suit to execute the Dance of the Fiery Flame, a scurrilous antic incited by the eggs probably, and politically, the less said about the performance and this episode in the history of my ship the better. Suffice it to relate that the ritual hinged on an out of date 'News of the World' newspaper rolled and stowed in a strategic position when it was ignited from the rear. Then a gyration of gargantuan proportions took place with leaps and bounds, which might have outdistanced Nijinsky, the final lap ending with the complete combustion of the newspaper. . . Rarely did the famous brew achieve this end result.

Chapter 5

The repairs to the ship continued, a long job. 'How long?' asked
Peter.

'God knows,' replied a perspiring Chief E.R.A. 'But I reckon at
least another couple of weeks and if I know my job, and I know
my job, when these . . . Who the blue blazes is that?' He broke
off to jerk a finger at a large Nigerian carrying a bundle of
dhobying along the boiler-room casing toward the forward
mess decks.

Ridley glanced in the direction of the strolling black man, 'Oh
there's a few of them forward Bob, each mess has engaged one
to do the dirty work and actually I'm thinking seriously of
getting one for us. How about it - willing to chip in a sou?'

In course of time there arrived ten or twelve of these unofficial
crew members who acquainted themselves with the parts of
ship, sleeping on the upper deck in nooks and crannies, gash
hands whose startling amenability secured a style of living for
the lower deck occupants bordering on the luxurious. Even the
wardroom hired a sort of gourmet cook who introduced a
succulent water-buffalo steak putting Alfie's ground-nut stew
rather in the shade.

The Nigerian Marine Dockyard completing repair, Columbine
was placed on Patrol Duties for a week, going out for a day or
two, returning to make a necessary adjustment. Lavis went

Stoker Les Harding, A. B. 'Taff' Reid and 'Gash Hand'

A. B. Johnny Lavall

down with malaria, so did Bains, and before long forty per cent of the crew were suffering if not the actual symptoms of malaria, were stricken with ear aches and head aches believed to have been brought on by the daily dosage of five grains of quinine; so it was providential maybe that the extra 'hands' were aboard. Lucky for the authorised personnel that is, certainly not the 'temporaries', because one day - probably 24th September - two hundred miles approximately from Lagos Columbine received instructions to proceed to Freetown forthwith.

Most embarrassing. Alfie sent for Lavis to ask him what was to be done about the Nigerians sitting despondently on the upper deck, but for once Jack could offer nothing in the way of advice or solution..

'Good Lord, we'll be putting them ashore in a foreign country!' cried Alfie, 'Why, they'll be hundreds - no, over a thousand miles from their homes! How the devil will they get back?'

All rhetoric, neither of them had the faintest notion of the answer; although Peppin <u>thought</u> he had when Bagsy told him of the conversation that had taken place in the skipper's quarters.

'Well, they all look alike, they'll get on all right' he sententiously remarked', not like Germans and us and the Frogs are they? Always tell them Germans can't you, by their square heads, and the Froggies wave their arms about a lot, the Eyties stand about singing all day, but these black fellows now, well you can't tell 'em apart can you? And how can they be foreigners eh? It's <u>all</u> Africa aint it?

It appeared that the problem was solved. But Turner had no time to make a decision one way or another because on arrival at Freetown they were at once put on escort duty and sent out with scarcely time to breathe. The second day out they came upon a merchant ship flying the French flag; nearby, a destroyer waiting, hove to. The Senior Officer of the Escort detailed Columbine to board the 'Vendome' to take a look at her cargo. The order came giving little opportunity for finesse, 'Doc' Rowlands in the W/T office was picking up wireless signals in plain language passing between the French destroyer and the Vendome as Maguire mustered the boarding party on the boat deck, a word repeated again and again that Coder Brian 'Icky' Thomas translated roughly as 'sabotage'. Maguire had been exhorted to make all possible haste which took the band of desperadoes climbing aboard the Frenchman clad only in singlets and shorts, brandishing pistols in their hands, while Dave Eatough swung a machine gun at the hip in tolerable imitation of Al Capone. This brought terror into the lives of the black crew huddled in the stern, eyes rolling in the approved Hollywood tradition. The Master exhibited excitable anger at what he called, in perfect English 'The unwarrantable invasion of his ship by a gang of cut-throat pirates'. Appeasing the man, Maguire made the suggestion they went below to talk it over and as he and the seeming affable fellow sat with a bottle of wine between them a signal came by light telling him to release the vessel. Ed shook hands, ready to go but stopped, aware that the Master had become so excited that he'd forgotten his English and grabbed him by the arm, pushing him toward the engine room.

'Look!' stuttered the poor chap, the palms of his hands turned up 'my engines are no good. They are all smashed. When we saw you coming to board us my engineers, they got . . . how you say . . . sledgehammers and some crow bars . . . What are we to do mon ami? We cannot move!'

Ed gave him a sympathetic nod, 'I guess you'll have to get a towrope on that destroyer out there. We can't do anything for you. We can't take you to Freetown because we've been told to let you go on your way. I'm sorry but it's au revoir. I wish you good luck' and K94's boarding officer left with a final hand-shake, his last glimpse of the Frenchman showing a figure weighted with problems bent over the taff-rail; another reminder that the war unlike lightening could and often did strike more than once in the same spot. The French at this time had almost as much to fear from the British as from the Boche. The conversation he had enjoyed and the wine offered was due to his nationality, not of his use of the English language for he had felt a genuine tinge of pity for the old man in the blue serge suit and when he climbed onboard Columbine he turned and waved again but the man had gone; maybe to drown his sorrows in many cups of wine in the listless ship, unaware that he would become a memory never lost.

On the heels of that miserable episode came another boarding with similar result. The political vacillation of Marshal Petain and quisling behaviour of Laval in Vichy France ensured sufficient pressure from the Admiralty when Ed Maguire found himself in this similar situation . . . out on a limb.

They had met a new, streamlined passenger liner of about fifteen to twenty thousand tons - a beautiful ship. She was called **'Eridon'** and the port of registration on her stern read, 'Marseilles'. The Senior Officer of Escort again detailed the 'gash-boat' Columbine to do the dirty work; again the finger was put on Ed to lead the party. Although he didn't actually say so, Turner had presumed Maguire was fluent with the French tongue by reason of it being Canada's second official language. Of course he was wrong, and Maguire swore in practised English when roused from his bunk at seven bells in the morning watch and told to muster on the boat deck with no time to clean his teeth. His boarding party this time consisted of four ratings armed only with rifles, and dressed with more circumspect than the last occasion, which had aroused awkward questions from the S.O. Additionally, there was a signalman with an Aldis lamp, and Charlie Bouswell went along as interpreter. Ed was given a large heavy pistol, extremely cumbersome, hanging from a holster which sagged to his knees to give him a walk with a curious waddling motion less suggestive of swash-buckling he couldn't imagine, and all he could see after the boat was lowered and he glanced back to

K.94, was a row of black faces - the press-ganged Nigerians-staring over the rail and cheering. The onlookers on the Eridon must have been puzzled by the odd craft with the singular crew, which had stopped them en route from French Indo-China.

Turner had said, 'When you get on board you're to tell the captain to proceed to Freetown, and that during the passage, you're to remain on board. And for God's sake Maguire, don't blast off your foot with that gun. Off you go.' Reaching Eridon the boat crew, used to the dimensions of Columbine, were awed by the immense structure and needed some skill getting aboard when Maguire asked to be taken to the Purser's Office and was conducted through a series of luxurious public rooms. Charlie had taken with him some copies of 'La France Liberte' and attempted to distribute these to passengers in the First Class Saloon, and had to be rescued from a middle-aged woman who spat at him, screaming that he was 'a bad Frenchman'. But, as Ed remarked to Palmer later, 'I was interested in some rather nice pieces of fluff flitting around and the sight bringing forth visions of living it up for a few days in the company of some good looking babes'. Asking the purser to produce the passenger list he stood running a finger down stopping to inject a note of suspicion as it rested on Monsieur Geller and Monsieur Schmitt.

'These are not French names?'

'Pardon Monsieur le Officier, ils sont Alsace.'

'Oh - they're from Alsace, on the border?'

'Oui.'

Maguire turned away, calling for his party to follow and made for the Bridge to find the Master. On the way they passed an officer coming down a companion-way who threw a quizzical glance at Bouswell then came back to speak in rapid French, the dialogue bringing the furious shaking of heads of both participants.

'What on earth was that all about Charlie?' asked Ed as they mounted the last ladder to the Bridge.

'My old Divisional Officer aboard the Tigre', Bouswell shrugged, 'He swore that he recognised me and if I accepted that he would inform my parents that I'm still alive. He comes from not so far from my village. But I had to persuade him he was mistaken, that I had a double maybe? It would have been bad for my people in the village, no one can be trusted in Vichy France today.' Stepping on the Bridge they found the Master flanked by sub-ordinates all standing rigidly to attention; he himself of spare build and of medium height, dressed in freshly laundered and pressed whites. Confronted by this immaculate group Ed felt like a slob in his unshaven condition with a pistol hanging down to his knees like a two-bit cowpoke and unconsciously over-playing his hand, his articulation a little too forced and meticulous.

'I have, Sir, instructions to order you to proceed to the port of Freetown and I and my party to remain on board during the voyage.'

The captain looked across to Columbine then faced Maguire to say in English, 'I shall not do it; I refuse.' Ed knew what he had to say next, but hesitated; it would sound so god-dammed dramatic if not ludicrous. Whetting his lips he raised his voice and said, 'Then I must shoot you!'

He saw the assessing gleam in the Frenchman's eyes and heard:

'Comme vous voulez' as expressive hands lifted toward him.

'What's that? What did he say?' he whispered to Bouswell who whispered back with a grin, 'Roughly speaking . . . Go ahead.'

Impasse? Not quite, for just then the signalman's attention was directed to answer the winking light from Columbine's signal lamp blinking a message to the effect they were to leave the **Eridon** and return onboard forthwith.

'Wow, that was close,' Maguire said in relief as his party pulled toward K.94,

'Wonder why we've been called back?

'Would you 'ave shot 'im Sir?'

'Don't be a clot Phillips.'

The S.O.E. had been in touch with the C-in-C. Atlantic about the boarding, but the 'Authorities' had feared reprisals on Freetown by Vichy bombers stationed in the nearby colonies. So Columbine acquired a new nickname. With the engine and rudder repaired she was no longer recognised as a jinx by her crew as Maguire quipped laconically in the wardroom that evening, 'We ought to be known as The Royal Abortive Borderers'.

Chapter 6

Columbine left Sierra Leone on the 5th October and was not to return until nineteen months had gone. The Nigerian 'Gash Hands' were 'demobbed' just prior to the leaving, where the old depot ship **Edinburgh Castle** rested on what many matelots thought to be thousands of empty provision cans, a bug-infested hulk. Across the harbour K94 needed to oil, and hatches were opened for the inspection to assess the level of fluid in the tanks - for these were not yet equipped with gauges. As the bolts were being withdrawn and the cover lifted, the inquisitive animal Jack Lavis had brought aboard five months earlier, leapt (or fell) into the hole. Pumping ceased to allow lengths of rope to be lowered in an endeavour to extricate the struggling animal whose screams for assistance and general ruckus brought Alfie to the corner of the Bridge in time to witness the bedraggled form brought forth held by a boat hook through its collar. Anxious as he was to get his ship on the move, Alfie leaned over, 'Ah, somebody throw a monkey into the works Mr. Lavis?' he called with malicious humour, a remark that Jack would never forgive . . . He loved that creature.

They were now part of the 6th Escort Group convoying to the North Channel. They completed re-fuelling at the island of San Miguel in the Azores, leaving Porto Delgada 16th October when, some time into the 'First' watch a signal instructed the Commodore to alter course; the convoy was to come South about and not use the North Channel. The diversion was quite inexplicable to Lavis at his usual First Watch duty with Trew because most convoys, and certainly on North Atlantic routes, convoys almost always used the Northerly Approaches and he gave an involuntary shudder as he remembered his last time in those waters. Literally.

Moments later, standing on the port wing of the Bridge there came a sudden explosion and a great pillar of flame and smoke emerged from a ship in the nearest column he recognised by her silhouette as the **Trevelyan**.

She was loaded with iron ore. The urgent voice of the Asdic operator came to him,'Contact Sir, Red four five, close, very close'. Jack had looked toward the interruption when it came then wrenched his eyes to the bearing given of the **Trevelyan's** position. It had gone; the vessel had disappeared - in a matter of minutes. He hadn't realised that he had pressed the Alarm bell, now Turner was on the Bridge, signalman McCall relieved from watch and sent aft to his Action Station, the yeoman, Drewry in his stead. Brazier stood ready by the Kleig searchlight situated behind the port Oerlicon.

'Switch on, signalman' called Turner.

Ted bent down and pulled the double-pole lever and nearly died. The thing would not focus at all, down to a fine beam that is, it just lit up the whole area, including Columbine, as if God had switched on the sun! 'What are you doing man!' roared Alfie, 'Get it trained on that U-boat!'

The U-boat, blowing all tanks was submerging as rapidly as it could but Ted couldn't see that, or wouldn't see that, as he hopped about thinking he was prime target without armour plate or even protective padding around the stupid blasted apparatus.

'I can't. Can't get it to f-f-focus Sir!'

The focus screw, a tiny afterthought, was embedded in layers of pussers paint which nothing would shift. Drewry brought gratitude from one source and a black mark from another when he anticipated by about two minutes Alfie's order to switch off. Of course, the submarine had by this time submerged anyway, and the corvettes preparing to drop depth charges, but the attack found no target, and while traversing the St. George's Channel when Turner had returned to his cabin, Lavis waited quietly brooding, waiting for midnight and the changing of the Watch.

'Do you believe in coincidences Trew? Do you think there's anything in what some people call pre-destination?' he asked, bringing a shake of the head from his companion and a 'No, not particularly, why?'

Jack pulled up his collar against the cool breeze, hoping they might get some of the hot 'kye' the gash-hand of the Watch was bringing to the look-outs. He dug in his pockets for a cigarette, 'Well, it strikes me this way, I'll tell you if you don't mind a bit of ancient history,' and he swore softly as he remembered he'd left his cigarettes below in a locker. 'I started my naval career,' he continued, 'on the Pomerol, but before that I was Second Mate of a Furness Withy boat called The Humber Arm. I was being paid eighteen quid a month and at the time didn't think it was worth my while to volunteer as a Sub-Lieutenant in the R.N. for only thirteen pounds a month. Anyway, there I was, on the *Humber Arm*. Bowaters owned her you know, the Paper people, and she was an ice-breaker - or at least equipped as such - and traded in newsprint mainly. She used to go down the Atlantic coast of America to the Gulf ports with this newsprint then usually called in at Galveston to load up with sulphur for the mills or, she would come to the U.K. with newsprint and <u>then</u> return with coal for the mills in Newfoundland. They were at a place called 'Cornerbrook' if I remember aright. Well the second voyage home we did the usual trip down to - New Orleans this time I think, not Galveston, carrying the normal cargo of newsprint, then went straight up to the mills, unloaded the stuff, took on board some steel, going on to Halifax to join a convoy to sail with a

Commodore whose orders were changed to bring him round the south of Ireland, and here's the nitty-gritty of my story: we were torpedoed.'

Trew looked up, his attention, which hadn't actually drifted, now completely concentrated. 'I say Jack, didn't know that - on your papers I suppose?'

'I suppose so, yes, surely it must be - anyway we were hit on the eighth of July last year; seventeen miles S.S.E of Fastnet, and that's not too far away from where we had that last set to is it. Providentially no one was lost, and we were picked up by the destroyer Scimitar and landed at Milford Haven. When I got home there was a letter awaiting from the Admiralty enquiring if I was still interested in a Naval career - or words to that effect - they followed it up with a telegram, and I thought, well, after that experience on the Humber Arm it'll probably be better to change my occupation slightly; to do the chasing rather than be chased.' He laughed nervously, finishing with, 'You know Tony, meeting the Trevelyan back there, in those waters, was rather like meeting a ghost.'

Their conversation drifted on a bit longer then the steps of their reliefs coming from below to take over the Watch cut short any further philosophic discussion as they said 'Goodnight' and prayed for undisturbed sleep.

Columbine arrived at Liverpool on the 26th October, berthing in the Albert Dock to undergo a five day boiler-clean at the end of which she went on ON convoys when she repeated her early days by escorting ships to nineteen degrees west then releasing them to a Canadian force, but the sudden transition from the tropics to the freezing rollers south of Iceland became an ordeal to her crew, creating sickness among them which after even the first trip, resulted in almost 30% of them getting back to Gladstone Dock having to be replaced as being unfitted for service in small ships. A few departed for courses leading to a higher rate.

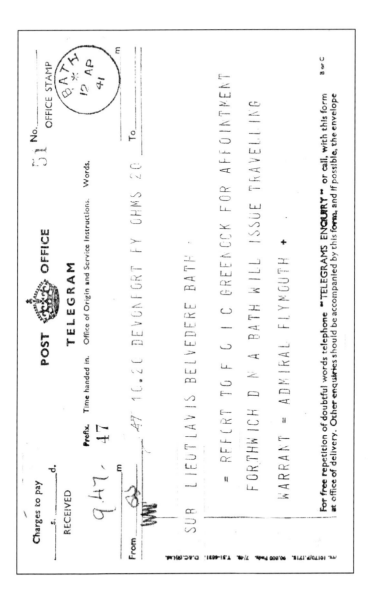

POST OFFICE

TELEGRAM

Charges to pay
s.   d.

RECEIVED

Prefix. 47   Time handed in.   Office of Origin and Service Instructions.   Words.

No.

OFFICE STAMP

BATH
12 AP
41

To

From

47 10.20 DEVONPORT FY OHMS 20

SUB LIEUT LAVIS BELVEDERE BATH -

= REPORT TO F C I C GREENOCK FOR APPOINTMENT

FORTHWITH D N A BATH WILL ISSUE TRAVELLING

WARRANT = ADMIRAL PLYMOUTH +

For free repetition of doubtful words telephone "TELEGRAMS ENQUIRY" or call, with this form
at office of delivery. Other enquiries should be accompanied by this form, and if possible, the envelope

B or C

Just before the second trip Jack Lavis was removed to hospital with a bout of malaria, which necessitated his 'Jimmie's' duties to be assumed by Ed Maguire who seized this opportunity to apply for promotion fully supported by Alfie. Then during November while the ship was undergoing repairs to engines overtaxed since the work done at Lagos, the repaired Lavis published on board the Banns of marriage for Bagsy Baker and his Molly, and Lieutenant Ed Maguire stood both the Steward and himself a congratulatory drink as he left to become the First Lieutenant of K.105, H.M.S.Loosestrife.

NOTE: When in Marseilles on his way to the train taking him, his wife, two children, and a lady secretary to Lisbon to open up the first Canadian embassy after the war, the taxi passed through the harbour. Alongside the jetty was the 'Eridon'!

Chapter 7

The new Asdic Officer picked his way through the Salthouse Dock to round the telephone kiosk and walk below the huge Jesse Hartley warehouses, with its tremendous iron columns like a Grecian portico along the side of Albert Dock where he had arrived, fresh from an anti-Submarine course up in Campbeltown, at the gang-way of his first ship.

'I'm the new Asdics Officer' he announced.

'Yes sir, been expecting you Sir,' acknowledged the quartermaster.

'Good. Get someone to show me to my cabin will you? I'd like to get this lot,' he indicated his baggage, 'stowed away as soon as possible.'

Fingering his Bosun's Call indecisively the Q.M. responded to the young man rather well; he said, 'Er . . .Your . . .eh . . . cabin Sir? Perhaps you should see the First Lieutenant, he'll know what to do'. Taking the newcomer to a ladder he pointed, 'Down there Sir, door on the right.'

The ship contained the habitual stink of oil and paint but for the young man it had a far more serious defect. It was utterly claustrophobic and he winced as he descended the short ladder to a door opening into what he took to be a cubby-hole but into which the builders had with amazing ingenuity managed to provide space for a bunk. An R.N.R lieutenant stood in the door-jamb on the point of leaving the mousetrap and extending a hand he smiled and said, 'Tuck?'

'Yes.'

The lieutenant smiled again, 'Lavis, Number One. Welcome aboard.'

Sub-Lt Graham Tuck made another statement, more in the way of observation, 'Small, isn't it?' he said, looking around Jack's cabin, 'Is mine the same size?' Lavis put up his hand to give a reflective tug to his nose, 'Ah, well, we have a small problem here Tuck . . . '

'Graham, my Christian name's Graham.'

'Well Graham, unfortunately there is at the moment only this one single cabin - which I occupy - and one other double which is being used by two other officers. It might be as well I think if I introduce you to the captain er . . . come along' He managed to squeeze past Graham, calling over his shoulder, 'Lt.Turner will sort you out.'

Alfie did. 'Tuck, eh?' he cordially welcomed the Subby, 'we'll soon have you fixed up', and to Jack he said, 'He can have my sea cabin Number One, young Palmer used it if you remember. He was quite happy with it I believe. Well then that's settled.' As Lavis moved away Turner addressed the Asdic officer again, 'Now I'd like a word with you about your duties and how I like to run my ship.'

Bagsy moved out of ear-shot thinking that Maguire's successor didn't look a bad sort of fellow and hoped Tuck and the skipper would hit it off together; it made life in the pantry so much more pleasant.

Graham quickly discovered that what might've been 'comfortable living quarters' for a certain Sub.Lt. Palmer was a positive inconvenience for Sub.Lt. Tuck. Since the 24th December when they had sailed on convoy he had found the tiny box was further restricted by the fact that he had to share it with Sub.Lt. Wills. Neither of them was in residence at the same time of course, they were doing Watch and Watch, but personal possessions had an aggravating way of becoming tangled up. That first night out was a lesson in fortitude as Columbine ran into a fierce northwesterly and the seas flooded over the foc'sle into their quarters below the Bridge tier. Coming off watch to find a foot of water sloshing about alongside the bunk, bailing it out, finding more when roused to take over duty watch again. He too had this baptism with the elements accorded to all who sailed in Columbine and sister ships, but he enjoyed the advantage, shared by Wills, denied their fellow officers; a bunk that was always warm.

A day or so later watching Trew with the sextant he asked the pilot if they were far from Hvalfiord, bringing a grin and, 'Don't need this thingummy to tell you that 'Pinger', take a look at your calendar; we arrive tomorrow.'

Tuck searched his pockets for a cigarette case offering it to Tony with the words, Tell me,' he said admiringly, 'Jack Lavis said that you got the ship on her first trip to Iceland by dead reckoning, and you navigated the ship to Freetown by star sight and arrived spot on. Is that true . . . er, Trew? Oh dear'. He tailed off as he realised the God-awful play on words, but Tony waved his apology aside, it happened so many many times he was bored by it.' Actually old man I went to a rather good school where they turn out gentlemen trying to be officers - and sometimes navigators - in six weeks, called His Highness King Alfred.' He laughed at Graham's look of disbelief, 'Sorry, that's Jack Lavis's description. But he's right of course, the tuition there is admirable, and yes, I'm quite proud of that achievement on my first trip to Freetown, I fancy not many others could do as much. Not even the pussers naval types eh?' The rhetorical question went unanswered in an unexpected gust of wind portending worse to come, and he hurried below to secure his movables in his shared cabin.

Leaving the convoy in the usual way and position, they put in at Hvalfiord, which is north of Reykjavik the Capital and here the weather broke and all hell was let loose as Turner elected that Columbine remained in the lee of the large tanker. A wise assessment of their predicament for they survived that wild night only by the judicious use of fenders and ropes, a nightmare of danger and effort later to play on the drunken nerves of one A.B. Bailey.

When daylight came most ships in harbour showed sign of having dragged anchors, some of them severely damaged. Telegraphists ashore were accommodated in Nissen huts with their apparatus, and one of these huts could be seen from he Bridge with its roof missing. Before they left for Liverpool with the **Camellia** and **Pimpernel** on New Year's Day 1942 the Communication Branch heard the apocryphal story that as the roof was torn off from the hut in which he was working, the 'Sparks' sent a signal to Headquarters that read: - 'Nissan hut airborne at 2230. ETA Reykjavik 20 seconds'.

Land-fall at Liverpool was made on the 7th January when they were diverted from Gladstone to the over-spill Albert Dock and leave given to the Port Watch. Polly Turner made reservations at the Stork Hotel, Trew remained on board but made frequent visits ashore, Lavis was able to go home to Bath, Brazier called on a cousin in St.Helens, McCall went to Cumnock, the Welsh contingent went to the hills, the Scousers were already at home and 'Brum'Bailey invited his oppo Les Harding and his oppo Ted Hateley to see his Mum.

Stepping out from the dock-yard gates, it was moved that they fortify themselves against the four hour journey on a steam train, with one or two alcoholic beverages at The Baltic, or maybe it was Tom Halls', so by the time they got to the top of Dale Street the Mitre presented an exceedingly Circe-like picture. Reluctantly forcing themselves from its embrace, the trio managed to stagger the few hundred yards to Lime Street railway terminus for a rocking ride which eventually, as the train drew into New Street brought the notion to 'Brum' to lower the compartment window and throw out his steaming bag as a fender to come alongside!

'You great flaming nit!' shouted Les as the bag teetered on the rim of the window, 'You're on a bleedin' train, not the bloody Columbine. Leave it where it is till we stop!' And he had presence of mind to wrench it from 'Brum's fingers. Outside they fell in with a nomadic tribe from the Salvation Army and Les, renowned onboard for his strong but not always mellifluous tenor voice augmented the choir with a few sharps and flats, a tremolo inserted now and again, here and there ad lib, while Hateley peered around the trumpets and trombones for any signs of the Viceroy's car. But tears were not very far away when the Army executed a final flourish on the castanets, in preparation to the move to the next pub, an idea that really did appeal to the lads, a Major bundled them into a number 29a omnibus with hurried instructions to the conductor.

They came back after leave. They all - officers and ratings alike, had this strange loyalty to their ship and their comrades, and Columbine sailed on the 14th January 1942 fully complemented. Another convoy to be taken to 19 degrees West, another battle with vicious winter, more days of uncertainty and fear to be disguised from each other. After a quick look into Lock Ewe on the 18th we were back in Liverpool on the 28th. Public houses along the Dock Road did a roaring trade, as did the Fleet Canteen in Gladstone Dock. Ship's postman Gilchrist went ashore to collect mail, signalman Brazier to collect AFO's, Turner attended another conference, Tuck a mini-exercise on Asdics in Derby House. Leading Telegraphist Eric Davis went to the S.D.O. in Gladstone Dock, met a First World War 'bunts', was taken home, and fell in love with the old 'Salt's youngest daughter. Five days afterwards, the conference Alfie had attended turned out to be Convoy ONS63 sailing from the Mersey on the 2nd January 1942, the escorts comprising the corvettes **Arbutus, Camilla, Columbine** and **Pimpernel**, and an American Lease-lend destroyer, a four-stacker now truncated to three and re-named HMS **Chelsea**.

The merchantmen were mustered, numbered, and put in station, and passing the Bar light vessel set course while the escorts took up screening positions; **Columbine** as always in the rear at Position 'S'.

Toward evening a signal was sent her instructing her to exchange stations for the night with the **Arbutus** who was sweeping the Port Quarter. Kier McCall who received this signal by lamp to give Lt.Wills, could guess no reason for this particular manoeuvre, he just assumed it to be another of those vagaries perpetrated by Senior Officers wanting to prove they could be Admirals directing the Home Fleet.

The change of position signal came again the following evening and thus looked very much as if it were to be an ongoing practice so when Brazier took over the Watch on the evening of the 5th February, he was ready for the transmission, and after passing it to the O.O.W., remained by the signal projector while K.94 and K.86 crossed paths. At that moment Ldg.Seaman Rousell came up to the Bridge; he was off watch and wanted a chat with his oppo Drewry, and he and the yeoman sat together on the low platform on which the starboard ten inch signal projector rested on its support, To make room for them, Brazier hoisted himself up to squat on the guard-rail, retaining balance by holding onto the S.P as he kept look-out and listened to the yeoman and his pal swapping yarns in quiet reminiscent tones.

The convoy was a mile or so off the Rockall Bank and as happens only occasionally in the North Atlantic, the wind subsided and the dark seas rolled past in a low and lazy swell; the slow twi-light overtaking them from the far side of silhouetted cargo ships poised as if on the edge of the world, the air uncannily still. The subdued conversation at his feet began to exercise a strange mesmerizing effect on Ted in this languorous sphere imperceptibly darkening as they steamed on into an enclosing mist, but he was jerked from this euphoria by the most peculiar sound. Not the least like an explosion or a thud, he thought, more like the noise the ship might make if she were being hauled through steel girders.

It was a strange sound, a weird sound, frightening, unsettling Drewry sufficiently to force him to his feet and exclaim, 'Tin fish!'

Alfie was on the Bridge about to return to his cabin after the receipt of the Night Station Keeping signal. Hearing Drewry, he came to the corner of the Bridge, and in a calculated manner said, 'Surely not yeoman. It didn't sound like that to me, not like a torpedo at all.'

Drewry banished discretion, he couldn't contain himself, his dislike of Alfie rose in his throat, 'How do you know? You've probably never seen or heard a torpedo fired in anger.' This insult caused Alfie to step back a pace possibly prepared to quote K.R's when 'Doc' Rowland's shaky voice filled the sudden stillness.

'W/T . . .Bridge . . .The Arbutus has just bought it in Position S for Sugar!'

The two antagonists stared at one another and the rest of the watch on duty stood silent and appalled as a series of quite definite explosions followed the shattering announcement. Then they heard the R/T directing Chelsea to close and investigate for possible survivors and to take these to harbour whilst other escorts continued with the convoy. U-136 got away unscathed to sink the Canadian corvette **Spikenard** on the 17th. Meanwhile the escort group rendezvoused with the American in-shore force, handed their charges over and accepted the east-bound convoy, bringing that back safely without incident; although the six U-boats operating west of the Hebrides were waiting for a repeat performance.

The Memorial Service held in the chapel was solemn, dignified; heroic in a way as the padre ushered in prayers for eighteen lost souls - lost to their comrades but hopefully not to God - and concluded by singing that marvellous hymn for seafarers beginning, 'Eternal Father, strong to save'.

When the service finished there was a pause before the raucous 'Get fell in' orders were bawled to take men back to their respective ships, and Tuck took shelter against the wall of the chapel using its protection against the wintry morning as he stood with Trew. 'You know,' he mused, 'a quite famous . . .well a favourite expression often used in church is, 'they who live by the sword . . .You must know it. Not much used <u>these</u> days, eh? It crossed my mind in there,' - he gestured - 'Prien, Prien of the U-47, sank **the** Royal Oak, then he got his come-uppence, sunk by the Arbutus and everybody said oh jolly good show, the Royal Oak has been avenged. Now the Arbutus has gone to the bottom, so has Prien been avenged? And does it go on and on, and d'you suppose <u>we'll</u> join the queue to Valhalla?'

Trew gave a little gesture of amusement,' You're getting as bad as Jack, Graham my boy, <u>he</u> was going on about pre-destination or some such the other day. No, there'll be no Viking funeral for us unless we make a mistake like the skipper of those chaps over there. Seems he thought he was going to be rammed by one of the merchantmen and switched on his navigating lights. What he saw was the submerging U-boat, the U-136.'

Signalman Brazier saw the two officers talking and thought he might grab the opportunity to satisfy his curiosity - no, not mere curiosity, it was greater than that, it was a need reaching into his bowels he thought - for he'd awaited throughout the sad and subdued ceremony for some chance to get closer to the Arbutus ratings. Previous to sailing on that fateful convoy, he had met, and made a friend of a fellow Cockney in Liverpool. He was a lad who had worked in New Zealand House in London as a lift attendant before the war, and had thereby been inducted into the New Zealand Navy. The two of them had arranged to meet again when the escort group came back from convoying, so now, stunned by the reading of the boy's name as one of those lost, Ted felt that he needed to know more about the disaster, and moved slowly over to the knot of survivors talking quietly in twos and threes, catching one of them by the arm.

'Look mate,' he said softly, 'Excuse me. Pardon me butting in like this, but can you tell me a little bit more about what actually happened? You see, I had a mate on board, and he's one who went down with the ship.' The rating turned, his voice still as low as were those of his shipmates, but with a compassionate yet relieved sort of edginess muttered, 'I'm sorry mate' then shifting completely round to face Ted, his voice took on a harder note.

'Yeah. I was in the After Mess Flat. We was playin' cards. Someone fought they 'eard a funny sorta bang, but no-body fought nuffin' about it until we felt the blinking ship lurch and dip backards like. So we drops wot we wuz doin' an' gets up top quick like, bloody chop-chop. All 'ell wuz loose up there; blokes wuz tryin' ter free the carley floats an' the whaler, an' I couldn't hardly <u>see</u> the Bridge, <u>or any of that part of the ship at all!</u> Then someone shouted that we'd bin torpedoed underneath where the Wardroom <u>wuz</u>, an' all that part of the ship on top of it, the C.O's cabin and the 'eads, wheelhouse an' W/T caboose, an' the upper Bridge, all that, fell in down frough the 'ole like yer guts fallin' frough yer arse. By this time I'd managed ter get in one of the carley floats an' was paddling fer dear life, but of course there wuz lotsa me mates splashing about in the 'oggin tryin' ter find somefink ter 'old onter until somebody came along ter rescue us. I fink I went a little bit faint then, 'cos next fing I sees is the poor battered K 86, an' she wuz foundering. She wuz sinkin' very quickly an' as she went I saw depf charges on the rails an' I fought Oh my Gawd, they're still primed! An' I started to shake like a bleedin' leaf. Well . . . I wuz lucky. When them charges got ter the depf they wuz set fer they all went off, an' arms an' legs, an' bitsa blokes went all over the place.'

He stopped suddenly, aware that Ted was near to tears, and then he went on talking, but slower, quieter, as though measuring his words.

'I don't fink the lads felt nuffin'. It would've bin quick an' all that. But it made me 'orribly sick an' I just sat in that carley finkin' that they didn't oughta 'ave them bloody depf-charges rigged fer firin' until yer goes fer action stations. Wot ship yer from china? The Chelsea?'

'No, responded Ted, 'I'm Columbine, K.94.'

The other man studied him awhile as Coxswain Ridley prepared to get his lads into line, and said, his eyes widening, 'By God you were lucky! Bloody lucky!'

'I know', Ted said slowly, 'I know.'

Chapter 8

On the 14th February they were off again, an extra man in the Asdic team, a Scouser with the unfortunate name of Dumbell, Thomas Dumbell. On reporting to H.S.D. Setherton prior to the sailing date, Setherton looked him over in the mess and said, 'O.K. where d'you come from?'

'Liverpool' replied Tom brightly.

'Ship! You clot, what was your last ship?'

'Oh . . . the Camellia.' Setherton's face brightened, 'Well that's something, she's part of our group - but you know that of course. Were you with her long?'

'Only a month; before that I was in destroyers - Vanoc, and the Westcott, I was a lot happier on them . . . more comfortable.'

'So you would've been with us when the Arbutus went down.'

'Yeah, I was lucky there.'

'You were lucky! Exclaimed the surprised Setherton, Don't you know we exchanged stations with her minutes before she was sunk? Could've been us? How d'you make out that you were lucky?'

'Easy. I came down from Dunoon to Vernon the Asdic Pool in Liverpool here and of course, it was 'up homers' for a day or two and this Jock came to keep me company while we waited for a ship. Didn't know his name then, just called him Jock naturally . . . like he called me 'scouse', Anyway, found it out later Shepherd. Then we were both called to the Drafting Office and the Master at Arms said he needed two Asdic ratings in a hurry, and told us to go and get our gear together and report back when he'd have the draft chits made out - ready like. Well when we got back I found that I had been drafted to the Camellia, he, the Scot, had been allocated the Arbutus. Little did the Master at Arms know he had handed out one of us a death warrant? In a few days the Arbutus was on the bottom, and Shepherd with her. It could've been me.' There was silence, broken by,' I reckon I'm lucky'

It was Columbine's penultimate convoy in the North Atlantic; there was to be one more, a fairly disastrous one as it turned out, but that was not to be until 1944, two and a half years further into the war. Meantime she moved into Sheerness to de-ammunition then following that, into the hands of ship repairers at Tilbury, or rather, Greys, to be more precise.

Able Seamen Coupe, Hainsworth and Wilfred Grey came by taxi directly chartered by the Admiralty although no one ever could elicit the reason for such emergency privilege for three Radar operators who actually left the ship nine months later. Except one, A.B.Grey, who remained as Navigator's Yeoman. Also retained was a dog, a terrier sort of thing, the only successor to monkey, mongoose chameleon, chicken, and parakeet, long since passed into the shades of their particular Valhalla's as Tuck would say, either by drowning, misadventure, or murder. The dog too was destined for immortality, bearing a name almost assuring that eventuality - Harlequin; Harlie for short, photographed with Peppin, Milton, Harding, Bruce, and Taffy Edwards at Tilbury.

For two months from 3rd March 1942 Columbine had civilians clambering all over her dismantling and re-assembling, adding and subtracting, an improvement here, a flourish there until the foc'sle was extended a few extra feet to give additional cabooses in the port and starboard passages. Tuck and Wills were delighted on their return from leave to find they could vacate their uncomfortable quarters for roomier accommodation, which were still small . . . but more congenial to the human frame.

While they were undergoing re-fit at Grays, the U-boat war in the Atlantic shifted its emphasis to the Western seaboard where the enemy were sinking ships before they could be made up into convoys for the escorts to bring across to the U.K., and on the day the Radar A.B.'s came to K.94 by taxi, the Admiralty also offered ten corvettes and their crews to the American navy. With them went twenty-four trawlers, and they arrived at New York in early March. The U.S. Chief of Naval Staff Admiral King was a forthright man who believed in America, and thought Britain had got it all wrong:

'They (the British) should make heavy attacks on submarine bases and building and repair yards' he said, 'thus checking submarine activities at the source and where submarines perforce congregate.' But in April he was compelled to accept what Britain had been saying for months, and instituted a system of convoying which became known as 'The Bucket Brigade', whereby merchantmen were escorted along the coast and tucked in for the night at safe harbours It was not however a satisfactory state of affairs in any way so Columbine was detailed to join another escort to be detached from Western Approaches, and, to proceed after re-fit to liaise with the Americans in the Caribbean, where her job would be to teach the United States Navy in the subtleties of convoy escort after Admiral King had finally submitted to pressure from both the British and his own countrymen, by the dreadful loss of tankers in that area. Close to a million tons of shipping had been lost; it was time to send in the Navy. So allocated to

Group B5, and that number bold on her funnel Columbine left Tilbury on the 2nd May after two months undergoing the re-fitting, gingerly feeling her way through that perilous area of the North Sea known as E-boat Alley, keeping one eye on the Admiralty Chart of swept channel and praying it was up to date, the other skinned to repel any sudden arrival of a German light assault craft. It grew dark, very dark, sooner than anticipated as mist swirled patchily around a watery sun, and by the First Watch when Lavis took over the Bridge and Brazier relieved McCall, the business of tracking from one buoy to the next was anything but easy. An hour went by; then both watchers caught the glint of a tiny unlighted craft seemingly secured to one of the buoys. This was a routine ploy of E-boats so they watched it with a certain amount of suspicion until Lavis growing ever more uneasy, called to Brazier standing by a projector, 'Use your Blue Lamp on it Brazier.'

Ted brought the Aldis from its stowage, flashing the 'challenge', expecting (yet at the same time apprehensively uncertain of getting) the correct reply.

'Try once more signalman' cried the anxious Lavis as he saw no answering flash coming from the small boat, and once more Ted directed the shrouded light toward the now suspected enemy having the same negative response - except that it now slipped from the buoy to head toward Columbine. Lavis leaped to the 'Action Stations' buzzer and pandemonium cracked open - shouts, the slamming of water-tight doors the scuffing of boots against ladders and Turner got to the Bridge just as Ted reported loud and clear, with a hallelujah in every syllable that it was an in-shore fishing vessel.

Turner swung on Lavis his face betraying a mixture of thwarted ambition, anger, and relief. 'A fishing-boat Number One? You jumped on the buzzer for a damn fishing-boat? My God, where were your eyes!' Brazier tucked his telescope under an arm and approached the officers who looked as though up to making challenges of their own and managed to take pressure off the situation by saying to Alfie that he too thought there was danger at the time the buzzer was hit, giving <u>his</u> version of the sighting. Alfie listened to Ted's conciliatory account then walked across to Jack Lavis who had meanwhile dismissed the hands from 'Action Stations' and was standing passively awaiting Turner's next move. Alfie had grown calmer, accepting that Jack had erred on the side of safety, but his super-ego now had him in thrall; like a terrier with a rabbit he couldn't let go, once committed to a decision or action or statement, it was his nature to push it forward. The sardonic devil within driving him on, he ordered Jack below, <u>HE</u> would finish the Watch and when Jack turned to leave, as if to rub salt into the wound he called, 'You won't be needing the binoculars Number One - hand them to the signalman will you.'

The wind roared at them the next day as they went through the Pentland Firth, and south by the Minches the seas began to roll the vessel and occasionally pat her back-side with something more than esteem or affection, gradually increasing its buffeting the further south they steamed until late in the afternoon Watch they sighted the headland of Northern Ireland at the entrance to Loch Foyle.

They turned the point to enter the loch; the weather seemed to abate almost immediately, and Columbine settled to a gentle roll when her bow ceased dipping. A few of the off-duty watch came top-sides to enjoy her entry into these calmer waters, most of them coming to Derry for the first time (K.94 was destined to have five visits in all) and they marvelled, as they were to always marvel at the loveliness of this approach, on this occasion the sun's rays were slanting down over the peat hills of Donegal and across the cultivated meadows standing to the water's edge. Dwellings wearing a gay, open-faced character uncluttered by blackout curtains dotted the countryside and a farm-worker or two halted in their labour to signal a greeting as the bow-wave crested along the shore. Shortly, the masts and funnels of a cluster of ships were noticed.

'Is that Londonderry? Small sort of place aint it? Said 'Tich' Evans (Asdic) from his viewpoint on the boat-deck, bringing a snort from his companion, H.S.D.Setherton. 'Course it aint' he replied in disgust, 'it's just an oiling station, can't you see they're mostly tankers? It's Moville. . Derry's about ten miles away yet, according to the Navi's yeoman. We'll stop there most likely to get fuelled up though. '

After securing alongside the ship's company prepared for the afternoon siesta, oiling was to be done the next day, The cooks of the mess were still below clearing the tables, washing the crockery, knives and forks, and some were engaged in making a 'duff' for tea. Radar operator A.B.Hainsworth lifted the 'fanny' of cold greasy 'dishing-up' water with the intention of dumping this 'gash' over the side, and made his way along the starboard waist hearing as he did so, a shout behind him in a European but definitely not English voice; swinging round he was astounded to observe the K.193 bearing down and a rating on board gesticulating wildly and obviously requiring Harold to seize Buttercup's back-spring or whatever. The radar A.B. had a definite problem. There seemed to be no-one else on Columbine's decks, what little he knew about seamen's duties was further clouded by the instructions hurled in his direction in what he concluded was French, or Belgian. There was no time left, the line came snaking toward him; the fanny clattered to the deck and the gash splashed out through the scuppers as Harold struggled and cursed, swore, prayed, and heaved; an unaccustomed ten minutes which left him 'flaked out'. He knew there ought to be a quartermaster and proper ratings on standby for this sort of thing and during the time of his travail he, when he had breath to spare between heaves and groans, promised himself that 'somebody's going to pay for this'. But, as he said to his oppo Wilf Grey afterwards,' How I managed it I haven't a clue and I'm too buggered to play hell'.

At Moville next day the re-fuelling was done while he and the hands came under the instruction of Buffer Frank Liss. The evening brought an almost incredible sight. There were lights, electric lights, and a fairyland of glittering colours as the beams from the shore reflected off the oily surface of the loch. It seemed almost indecent as they recalled that just across the channel, barely three hours steaming away lay a city, an entire country, in total darkness with people - relatives, friends - shuddering beneath the onslaught of Hitler's blitzkrieg. Above them the moon showed a benign face. An impossible charade is this world grumbled Wills to himself as he went to the cabin he shared with Tuck. It had been cleaned and tidied by the new rating Dumbell and his bunk looked inviting after the long day on watch, and as he drifted away he idly speculated and to no great purpose on the possibility of a new First Lieutenant. The latest incident between Alfie and Jack made it clear that someone would replace Lavis at the earliest opportunity and it seemed likely that Derry would be the place for the purpose, before they were committed to the long commission on the other side of the Atlantic. He knew Alfie rather liked Tuck, but . . . he yawned and turned over, 'What the hell does it matter anyway, I am going home. When we get to the States maybe I'll get to call on my folks in Boston'

As he made his way forward to his own hammock Tom Dumbells face wore a beatific grin. His new duties looking after the officers had brought him in contact with the P.O. Steward, and a sort of friendship had sprung between the Welshman and the Scouser which had nothing to do whatever with the glass of gin given him by Peppin, of course.

The Pilot came aboard the next morning, a middle-aged, square featured Irishman climbing to the Bridge striving not to look like a civilian, with a peaked cap and an air of straining authority as Turner handed over control for him to manoeuvre through the Narrows and into the River Foyle.

What a gracious passage this was too, especially after the first bend when the river ran straight for about three miles, its banks no more than two hundred yards apart. As the ship glided swan-like along the placid stream it sometimes appeared as if Columbine was on stage, taking part in a fantastic play by Materlinck or Strindberg; the high banks festooned with wild flowers, brilliant clumps of rhododendrons, and copses full-throated with the call of birds and all practically within arm's-reach from the Bridge or gun-whale. White-washed cottages surrounded by neat walled gardens intruded one tiny wooded area where trees with the fresh young green of Spring hung their leaves over the water like some vast and mysterious proscenium arch; while all the time, odours and scents from these deep woods filled the narrow channel to beguile senses and to make all on board feel as though strife no longer existed and that they travelled to the haven of peace.

Alas, Londonderry was, and is, not like that. It was a wild yet curiously circumspect, bustling town of taverns and tangled wires and ropes littering the quayside, where escort vessels moored and departed daily on duties with convoys, or on coastal exercise.

Here Lt. Jack Lavis conducted Lt. Jackson around the ship, passed a few words of advice to the new 'Jimmie', and with a final salute to the quarterdeck relinquished his responsibilities.

Here the ship remained, with periodical essays into the waters north of Ireland with their sporadic intervals of cloud, rain, wind and sun, as they tested engines, tested guns, tested men.

Here, among the true Irish of the crew, McCarthy, the 'Jack Dusty' won the exchange with goodies from the ship's stores and those from his native Eire whose border needed but a step to cross.

Here, on the 23rd May 1942 Columbine left to rendezvous with a west-bound convoy and leave the Emerald Isle in the familiar bluster of a Force Five gale.

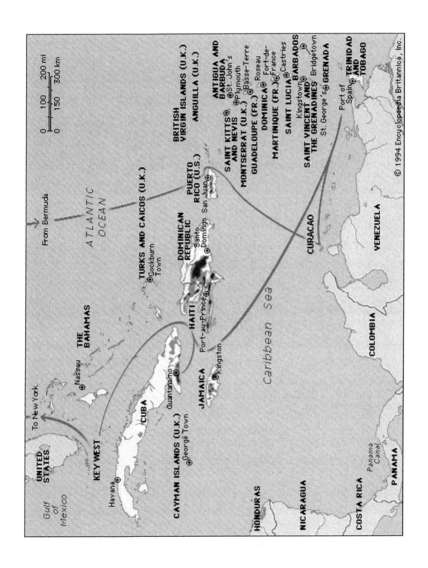

Chapter 9

The date was the 23rd May 1942. Turner sailed with half a dozen extra members in his crew; his officers were the new Number One Jackson, and Tuck, Mackie, Wills, Trew, and Wallis replacing Palmer, and on the 28th he wrote to Polly:

'We sailed straight into 5 days of gales & the ship has been too lively to do any writing, - she is still kicking about but not so badly. This weather was somewhat surprising after the lovely spell we've had &, I think, very annoying to some of our people, especially the new ones who have been extremely sea sick! However they are all getting over it and, no doubt, will be all the better for it. This is jolly bad luck really, Pet, seeing it's getting toward Mid-summer and might reasonably expect some fine weather. - I tell my officers that there must be a Jonah among them.'

Arriving at Newfoundland K.94 was shunted to the new base created by the Americans at Argentia, and there boarded by a small party of Yanks who fitted a sort of Semtex non-skid compound over the steel plates of the foc'sles which was, twenty-six months later to give the death-knell to one rating and to injure another - strangely enough, when Columbine was under the command of an American war-ship.

They were placed in what the U.S. Navy designated as 'Task Force 90 point', although the British concept of the three destroyers and nine corvettes as Group B5 ensured the retention of that number on their funnels, and found when they got to Bermuda they were to be split into three operational

**Bruce, Phillips and Nuttall
at Key West**

Jackson and Tuck
'An overnight stop at Puerto Rico'

units. With Columbine was the Belgian corvette **Buttercup**, the Canadian corvette **Snowberry**, an American P.T. boat while the Senior Officer was the destroyer **Warwick** under the command of Cdr. Cleeves who had left the **Clematis** for promotion. All officers and all men from all ships enjoyed the hospitality of the island, being feted by the W.H.O. (Women's Hospitality Organisation) ensuring not a wink of boredom would arise during their stay; until one blot appeared on the escutcheon of K.94.

Leading Seaman Ken Rousell - one-time fisherman from the Channel Isles - had been 'made-up' to Petty Officer and had moved aft to reside in that mess, and, I suppose in way of celebration went ashore with his friend Drewry on the very day that Lt. Graham Tuck went ashore to make the most of a beach party by 'crystal clear warm water' at Somerset, an island paradise across the Great Sound five or six miles from the capital Hamilton, and was summarily invited to the Court House as a character witness for the rating in rather warmer water who had 'filled in' the Governor's son. Graham's diplomacy paid off; Ken spent one night in clink.

For the officers there was in fact rather too much entertainment for the local notables vied with each other in the giving of brilliant parties, If cocktails were mentioned on one invitation card then the next one was certain to indicate champagne-cocktails. There was also, the 'danger of the heiresses' when word got around that certain of the young ladies on the island were looking for marriage and would bring substantial dowries to their bridegrooms, and Alfie was astounded to hear the figure £30,000 mentioned!

He thought it expedient to sound a note of warning to the young officers in his care to the effect that the answer to any requests for permission to get married would be 'No!' He argued that if an officer fell genuinely in love it would not harm him to wait until a more opportune time for marrying. If however he had largely fallen in love with the dowry he had no business to get married at all. There were no serious casualties in Columbine.

After an over-night stop at Puerto Rico they made landfall at Willenstad, Curacao, on the 18th June creating a bit of a furore when liberty-men stepped ashore in tropical rig. The native inhabitants had never before seen white men clad in shorts!

The island, about thirty-six miles off the coast of Venezuela, is rocky and barren, of volcanic origin, the harbour constructed out of an enormous extinct crater which was land-locked until a channel or canal was driven through from the south coast to let in the sea when the town began to take shape alongside this water-way some little distance from the oil storage tanks the principal source of the Dutch island's economy. While on her first visit, there were to be several as she plied the routes between Trinidad and Key West, the townspeople were awakened by the sound of gun-fire, and shells audaciously lobbed by a U-boat to drop among these tanks. On the way to Trinidad two or three days after this Sub Lt Wills was sifting through mail in his capacity of censor.

'I say Wallis, here's something!' he said, 'what shall I do about this? Is it contravening the rules about censorship do you think? Here, let me read it to you - it's written by that radar rating we picked up at Tilbury.'

'I had been to the S.A.Canteen and had a sandwich and decided to take a mosey around the town because it's Dutch you know and has got some very nice houses away from the oil refineries. I was making my way back to the ship when up comes this big Dutch fellow, and he was quite big, and I don't know why but he suddenly started to tell me that he and another chap, another Dutchman, were put ashore by the U-boat that shelled the town yesterday, and while they were onboard the sub, he saw a newspaper six months old which implied that the boat had been away from Germany for six months.'

'Wow! . . .what about that?'

'Definitely a contravention - You'd better have a chat with this rating - er, what's his name?'

'Coupe. Yes. I'll, do that as soon as I get through this little lot.' and sure enough he collared Bob in the wheelhouse.

'Look here seaman, you could be in serious trouble with this' he said, waving aloft the aerograph, 'if it got into the wrong hands somebody could put two and two together and find out something that could bring down danger to all of us, not just us but all the ships in our group!'

Bob himself couldn't understand why he had written in that way because in previous letters he had never even commented on the weather for ten days after because he'd read somewhere that reports in the newspapers were done that way.

'I'm sorry sir'.

'Very good - I'm afraid I'm compelled to destroy your letter Coupe, so you'll have to write another. Within proper bounds, do you understand?' Wills was pleased that he had admonished the rating without too much rancour; Coupe was pleased that he had been let off the hook so lightly.

Getting to Port of Spain, Trinidad in early July the group began a series of escort duties taking them over the next four and a half months between the Caribbean ports, with one voyage in the latter days up to New York and back imposing much strain on the entire crews as they passed rapidly from one temperature to another in either direction. It was at Trinidad that Ted Brazier my chief informant was made up to the rate of Trained Operator (sig). Among the numerous apocryphal stories of K94's sojourn in the West Indies is one that relates the exploits of a number of matelots boarding a tram, taking over the driving position and going through issuing make-believe tickets from make-believe machines to the amused passengers. Many instances of similar quality lie locked in the memory of those unfortunately not now living and who had no thought to tell me. On a more sober theme Lt. Tuck remembered taking off from Port of Spain for Key West Florida, steaming approximately north-westerly about eight hundred miles across the Caribbean leaving the picturesque string of the Leeward Islands to Starboard which brought them to the Old Bahamas Channel having passed close to Jamaica to Port, and in another hundred miles or so Cuba, again to port, with the black frowning mountains of Haiti to Starboard. 'We almost expected to see a pirate galleon bearing down on us wearing a skull and cross-bones at the Yard rather than the sinister dark shape of a U-boat.'

It was during this passage, and others, that many alarms were raised; the crews shocked into action, forever on 'top line', though no ships in their charge were ever lost.

Alfie Turner made it a prerequisite to write something every day to be posted to his wife as soon as his ship tied up: -

Although Columbine with her sister ships in each convoy undertaken sustained no loss, things were very different further north. There was one time when K.94 was heading for the U.S.Cuban Base at Guantanamo and in range of R/T broadcasts from the escorts coming from the Hudson River (New York) south to Cuba. They heard the transmission: 'Am in contact with enemy U-boats!' and later, from a Canadian corvette, 'Am intending to ram!'

On reaching Guantanamo Brazier learned that the corvette having 'pinged' a contact, dropped depth charges and brought a U-boat to the surface, then turned and rammed it but in so doing, ripped her Asdic dome from her hull. The Senior Officer of Escorts came to assist, designated another escort vessel to take charge of the convoy and accompanied the corvette with her bunch of German ratings on board to reach

13. Saturday, 19/9/42. Dearheart, - I've just come down from two hours on the bridge during which I careered about all over the place. - We contacted something at 5000 yards, so I closed it up, full speed + soon made out a tiny shape through my glasses. - It looked just like a Jerry + I went full at it + was very close when it hastily flashed a morse lamp, - I headed to just clear it + it turned out to be a tiny patrol launch - it has a most unfortunate silhouette for its own safety, + if it hadn't flashed, I should certainly have rammed it. - As my Yeoman of Signals said "judging by the quality of its signalling we gave it a great fright." - By that time I was several miles from our lot + so went back at full speed, - two of them were badly out of station so I ran close alongside them + told them to get back again by loud-speaker - + then I came down here to write to my darling, - I don't think it will matter my giving you this little account as I've divulged nothing of a secret

Alfie's Letter

Trained Operator (Sig) Ted Brazier

Guantanamo the day previous to Columbine's arrival. The skipper of the Canadian corvette received a severe 'blast' from the Admiralty for losing an Asdic dome, which could not be replaced in that area. The American S.O. received a commendation.

Guantanamo hadn't much to commend it from the point of view of the Lower Deck, although Tuck and Alfie were able to engage a boat and a skipper to go fishing for murderous barracuda.

Plenty of small Yankee ships frequented the harbour - indeed they frequented more than any sea-time they did, and appeared to live the life of Reilly with film shows on the upper deck, washing machines, drying machines, ice-cream. Once, a signal came winking at K.94 coming alongside: 'One Petty Officer and one rating from Warwick, one rating each from Columbine, and Buttercup and Snowberry. All A.A. Gunnery ratings will report to A.A.Training Site 1400 hrs today'. When they came back it was learned that no instruction or practice had been given them. They had cleaned the latrines! However good news of a sort came aboard the next day with instruction that instead of Key West they were to escort a convoy to New York. As they had recently been granted American rates of pay while in harbour and normal pay while at sea the prospect raised spirits no end; until it became apparent that this extra 'boodle' was to be held 'in trust' and they were to get 'hand-outs' on entering port of ONE TWO-DOLLAR BILL. Naturally leading to the practice of scrounging from the civilians when they got to 'The Big Apple'.

New York was exciting for everyone. The hospitality wonderful, invitations abounded - baseball games, American football, theatre, opera, dancing, restaurants and bars. The first thing Ted Brazier and his regular oppo Eric Davis did after the ship berthed at Pier Six on Staten Island was to catch the ferry to Manhattan. Wanting to see the 'Sights' they were directed to the subway and told to ask for Times Square, and here met the first snag - they had no coins to operate the turn-stile. Just then an American called, 'Hey Mac, c'mon!' and shovelled enough coins in the slot to allow all three to pass through then moved off before the friends could thank him. This was their initiation to living on their wits.

They gawped at the Empire State Building, Radio City, Madison Square Gardens, Jack Dempsey's Bar, made acquaintance with three elderly women of Scottish extraction who, concerned about their youth (Ted was twenty-one, Eric nineteen) and that they were so far from home, took them to a 'slap-up' meal and gave their addresses in New Jersey with insistence that the pair make contact next time or whenever their ship came again.

Usual routine was to call in at the White Ensign Club in Manhattan to peruse the notice board, which carried invitations to private addresses where one could spend a day, a night or weekend - given permission from Commanding Officers. There were free tickets to most of the shows on Broadway, and there was always the fun of a free meal at the Stage Door Canteen when servicemen would be handed a sandwich by James Cagney, cup of coffee by Ann Sheridan, a packet of fags by Alan Ladd then sit to eat in the company of Benny Goodman, Peggy Lee (a young lassie then), The Ink Spots; with chorus girls and starlets as hostesses. Once, like something from a later Hollywood film about three sailors loose in New York, Ord.Telegraphist Malcolm Salisbury went with them for a free lunch at the Stage Door but warned them that he'd have to leave around half five because Anna Neagle was to pick him up at that time. Naturally Ted and Eric thought this sounded like one of the tall stories habitually coming from Albert Troops, so they hung about outside until five thirty when sure enough right on time the limousine drew up and Malcolm got in.

With all such munificence abounding it's not surprising that some of the crew wanted a lion's share - or in one instance, a jackal's share. The bearded Jan Gatehouse contrived to get a certain asdic rating put 'in the rattle' and to be awarded fourteen days Number Elevens. Meaning extra evenings work, each evening. There being a land-line from ship to shore, the certain rating telephoned the certain starlet to explain his absence and was kind of rattled when the phone was answered at the other end by . . . Jan Gatehouse!

As 'Doc' Rowlands remarked the first time they left New York, as he looked at the skyline disappearing from sight astern, 'I can't believe it Ted. It's like stepping out of the front row of the cinema stalls and through the screen.'

The convoy south was uneventful; Turner caused lines to be out rigged to entice a marlin or barracuda when weather permitted, stopping engines to investigate when necessary and giving unrest to those expecting a tin fish to strike, then, on a return trip to Florida from Cuba, two or maybe three days from landfall at Key West, they chanced upon a lone Liberty ship.

She exhibited no sign of life; neither did she make any response to the signals made to her by the S.O. Escort. Columbine was detailed to 'vet' her so closing and circling Alfie bawled questions through the loud-hailer to no effect, and finally mustered a small boarding party and sent them off to find that the vessel's life-boats were gone and davit ropes trailing.

The sea was calm, the visibility was clear; and the ship rolled imperceptibly cradled in a weird lullaby as the boarders climbed over rails to silence. Not a soul aboard, but unfinished meals on the tables, some clothing in lockers left open, little obvious damage. Somebody muttered something about the Bermuda Triangle and the Marie Celeste and was told to 'Shut up' as they disbanded to look through passages and divisions more efficiently; when it became evident that unlike the Marie Celeste, this crew had left in their own life-boats. The big question was, WHY?

Cdr. 'Mac' Cleeves quickly made up his mind to have the vessel towed and instructed **Buttercup** to also put a party on her, causing the Belgians to man the winches with some alacrity as they thought of all the salvage money coming their way. The ropes being secured **Warwick** began the tow, when above the noise of her engine and the swish of the stricken ship's bows through the water a horrifying kafuffle ripped through the sea from below and the ship dropped at least three feet - like a lift out of control - to settle deeper in the water. Surely it was taking in the sea from some undiscovered hole? But the tow continued as the possibility of a torpedo hit was considered. Then another ominous sound echoed around and within the ship and the dual-tongued boarding party separated out to close all the watertight doors they could locate, in the firm hope that the ship would survive and reach Key West. A third cataclysmic roar reached the ears of Alfie on Columbine's Bridge and not waiting for orders from the **Warwick** flashed an order for her party to leave immediately. No second telling, they came; not so the Belgians despite the official order from the S.O., waiting until the decks on which they were standing were almost awash and only then rowing back to Buttercup amid cheers from their shipmates.

Key West lies at the end of a group of islands stretching westwards from the tip of Florida and is of course an American base. For Graham Tuck it was home to the biggest T-bone steaks he'd seen in his life, for Eric Lionel Davis, it was the finest and rarest of hamburgers. Instead of canteen messing they were put on Yankee Victualling, which meant that after a week of those rations, enough was left in the mess to last another fortnight. But when the Pusser Paybob at Trinidad heard of this arrangement through the loss of the usual 'rake-off', Yankee Victuals became unsuitable for British palates and a return was made to Canteen Messing, viz - 1s/10d per day per man and good old corned dog.

There was another convoy to New York, arriving on the 18th December from Pointe Noire, when everybody anticipated spending Christmas supping up the festival spirit at the Stage

Door Canteen and elsewhere, but they were disappointed - set to sail on the 21st December for Newfoundland and England. The money held back from the Caribbean was paid allowing a rush to Kessler's Stores on Statten Island to spend it all to the last half-penny, aided by young ladies called in by Mr. Kessler to advise the British lads on purchases required for young ladies at home. He afterwards supplied a bottle or two, or more.

Before going however a number of Columbine's ratings went to a Brooklyn cinema to see a film about Welsh miners - most of her crew at this time being Welsh - called 'How Green Was My Valley' in which is depicted in a minor part (a minor miner in fact) a short stocky chap who is a bit of a boxer look you, with a belligerent manner matelots call 'stroppy' and this character was recalled to mind several months later when Columbine got her second commanding officer.

The journey north to St. Johns was ghastly, the Hudson River was very close to freezing over, and mooring ropes were literally chipped off the bollards. Christmas Day was spent at sea. On the 28th December they had taken station on the east bound convoy in a dense fog that persisted for the next two days, and on New Years Day Tuck awoke with a monumental head-ache due to a poker game the previous evening leading to several gifts of rum as he went through his repertoire of risqué songs. The escorts for TM1 were the destroyer **Havelock** and the corvettes **Buttercup, Camellia, Gentian, Godetia, Pimpernel, Saxifrage,** and **Columbine.**

Yeoman Percy Drewry left the ship on arrival in Liverpool losing his life shortly after on a Russian convoy. His position was later taken on by Ldg Sig Burnett. The 'Jack Dusty' McCarthy also went to another ship and his duties taken over by Seaman Wilkinson. The date was the 13th January 1943 as K.94 underwent a boiler clean. On the 4th February, Sub. Lt Michael Ball replaced Tony Trew the navigator. Bob Mount who formed one third of the first radar trio departed as a C.W. candidate. Peppin also left at this time.

Operating out of Londonderry they found themselves en route to Gibraltar and almost immediately on arrival Turner issued orders to paint ship which was done while he and Sub Lt Mackie took off to fish for red garnet; and on the following day when Turner attended the sailing conference the last lick of grey was wiped over the stern. Sunday the 28th was heavy with rain as Brazier hoisted the flags requesting permission from Capt.D to leave harbour. The corvettes of the 38th Escort Group, **Anchusa, Coreopsis,** and **Jonquil** slipped at the same time and because the **Aubretia** remained at her berth undergoing a minor repair, the trawler **Loch Askaig** and the ancient V&W destroyer **Vanoc** were seconded to the group and detailed to take the convoy XK2 northwards. Beyond The Mole in the Straits the thunderstorm broke and the rain lashed down all that day until the evening when the wind took over to reach gale force. The twenty merchantmen kept up a steady rate of knots however, rounding Cape St.Vincent when the stern wind allowed them to maintain eight knots, all in station.

At 2330hrs March 1st the make-shift detector contacted a U-boat on the surface 3000 yards away Mackie pressed the alarm buzzer and called to Turner, 'Captain Sir, U-boat on the surface, 3000 yards away, have altered course towards it Sir!'

As he reached the Bridge Alfie heard the lookout cry,' I think she's seen us Sir, she's turning away towards the convoy.'

'What's her range now?' snapped Alfie.

'About 1300 yards Sir' replied Mackie.

'Right. I want gun's crew closed up, have them fire a star-shell, give our position and speed to the S.O. and say we're going in to attack.'

As the star shell illuminated the area the U-boat could be seen ahead blowing its air tanks. Alfie wheeled on Burnett, 'Yeoman, get a search light on it will you - pronto man, as quick as you can.'

The distance between the adversaries rapidly closing with Columbine making sixteen knots, only gave time for the shaft of silvery light swaying over the heaving black waves for the observers on Columbine's Bridge to read the number on the conning tower before it slid below the surface . . .U-445.

'Damn, damn, damn, swore Alfie, 'reduce speed; we'll have to rely on the asdics though I doubt very much that anything will be found in this swell. Tuck lad, carry out a sweep between compass bearing 010 and 090.

The sweep continued throughout the next hour with different bearings but as Alfie had suspected, with no success, and with the convoy getting further and further distant he realised that he ought to abandon the search within the next thirty minutes to enable him to regain station by morning light. Reluctantly he gave the order to resume original course, during which time the weather began to moderate bringing fine sunny conditions on the Wednesday, when a Focke-Wulf dropped out of a clear sky to take a look at them. All the escorts, and one or two of the merchant ships equipped with anti-aircraft guns took pot-shots at the enemy plane but the pilot kept at a safe distance and evidently was only there to chart the course of XK2. Because next day they were visited by a Focke-Wulf - possibly the same one - accompanied by a high-level Dornier 217 which loosed its bombs all of them missing except one that hit the 4765 ton Chateauroux; fortunately not exploding.

Watching this and as the planes flew off, Mackie whistled,' Gosh Sir, that was lucky!'

'Maybe', countered Alfie, 'but I fear we'll be in for it tomorrow when those blighters make their report to wherever they're stationed. The Admiralty signals say there are up to ten U-boats in this area and I'll bet you anything you like that they are aware of our situation right now.'

He lit his cigarette for the fourth time and drew on it with slight distaste as a shred of 'tickler' stuck to his lip.

'I'm off below. I'll be up before it gets dark, but if anything happens meantime . . .'he broke off to tap the voice-pipe.

The convoy continued on its northward course throughout the remainder of the day, and the night without molestation, and through the next day too until, just off Vigo unchecked by the screening escorts, U-130 made contact and managed to put herself within the extreme limit of visibility and there she submerged and waited to attack at dusk.

At precisely 1750hrs tremendous double explosions echoed over the calm sea from the starboard side of XK2 and the appalled Watch on Deck saw the 5300 ton **Trefusis**, and the **Empire Tower** of some 4400 tons rapidly sinking. The U-130 had stationed herself directly in the path of the oncoming ships to release a salvo of torpedoes from her forward tubes; she then swung round to fire a stern salvo as she took evasive action. The first torpedo struck the **Ger-Y-Bryn** bringing the 5108-ton vessel to a limping halt with clouds of smoke billowing in the air, boats and rafts being thrown hurriedly over the side. The second missile crashed into the smaller 1574 ton **Fidra**. She went down in two minutes!

A flurry of signals put the convoy on an emergency turn of 95 degrees to Port as the **Anchusa** and the trawler dealt with the rescue of 102 survivors from the holocaust, Columbine, **Jonquil** and **Vanoc** continued with the escorting while the **Coreopsis** made unsuccessful depth charge attacks By 1820hrs it was all over, sixteen thousand tons and many irreplaceable lives went down in half an hour without hindrance as the remainder of the convoy steamed onward waiting for the next hammer, the next blow against an inadequately protected hull.

The first breath of relief that they themselves had escaped came from a thousand throats as prayers were uttered on the Sunday, filling the air from every remaining ship in that convoy; a toll for the brave, a benediction for the lost souls, litany for the living, rosary, breviary, bell book and candle.

The second breath came at the welcome sound of a rising sea, and the full roar of a Catalina flying overhead as the convoy headed into the sector patrolled by R.A.F. Coastal Command, and the next two days were free of attacks although it was known that sixteen U-boats were skulking around. Gale-force winds and limited visibility caused by frequent rainsqualls offered them partial cover as they drew nearer to the Northern Channel where Columbine and the other escorts dispersed XK2 and proceeded up Lough Foyle to Londonderry.

On Thursday March 11th was a conference ashore to analyse the U-boat attacks of the voyage, then Turner went on a short leave during which an Admiralty summons revealed that he was to take command of another ship.

Getting back to 'Derry at the end of the week he received written instructions to escort a tanker to the Clyde then to steam down to Belfast for re-fit.

The ship cast off on Saturday 20th with the usual pilot on board to negotiate Columbine past the treacherous sand banks. Hands were at their laid-down stations for leaving harbour; on the Bridge were the lookouts, signalmen, the pilot, Lt.Tuck, and Alfie, who wheeled suddenly from the pilot's side.

'I've been transferred!' he announced in a low voice, the hurt welling in his throat as he fully realised that at last he really was going to lose his 'dear ship', this time for good not just a temporary measure as it was with the **Amaranthus** in '41. He swallowed and tried again, 'I'm to go to Montreal to take command of one of the new River Class frigates there, H.M.C.S. **Evenlode** . . . river on the Thames isn't it . . . above . . .Oxford?' His voice tailed off as first Jackson, then Mackie followed by Tuck offered congratulations. Five minutes went by as navigational instructions were given by the pilot and passed by the captain to wheel-house and engine room, who then glanced toward Tuck. 'Er, would you care to come with me Tuck? As my First Lieutenant? I think that I could arrange it if you would like . . .'

Graham looked up with a grin,' Absolutely delighted Sir, absolutely, thank you.' He replied, little knowing a similar situation would later occur fictitiously in a novel by Nicholas Monsarrat.

They reached Belfast on Sunday 21st May 1943 On the Monday Lt.Jackson left to take his own command, another 'Flower'. Steward Peppin departed, so did others of whom I've no record. The Gunnery Officer James Riley came aboard at the same time as the mast was removed and re-sited abaft the Bridge. Before going, Alfie arranged for a group photo to be taken of himself and his officers. Wallis, Tuck, Himself, Jackson, Mackie, and in front the new Navigator, Sub.Lt. Michael Ball. On Tuesday the 23rd. Lt. W.J.Griffiths stepped aboard H.M.S.Columbine and relieved Alfred Lawrence Turner who with much regret but with a final flourish made a speech to the men and was rewarded with three cheers.

Columbine settled down to a major re-fit, and her second phase.

Back: Wallis, Tuck, Turner, Jackson, Mackie. Front: Ball

Chapter 10

Lt. Griffiths strode up the gang-way to make his way forward dodging the hoists and tackle of the dock-yard matees swarming all over the ship, to the paint locker in the foc'sle, finding A.B.Tommy Carr busy with a wooden model of Columbine half finished in his hands.

'Put that down and get your brush' he ordered brusquely, 'I require the letters O.B. to be painted in white on this'. He produced his steel helmet and finished with, 'It should take only a few minutes . . . I shall wait.'

The job done he next climbed to the wardroom to introduce himself to the officers under his command with the words, 'Gentlemen, I am your new captain. I do not know what your recent commanding officer expected, but I expect discipline and expect to get it. If I find any slackness on the part of any rating in this ship they will discover the letters on this tin lid fully justified. They mean gentlemen, 'OLD BASTARD.' During the next six months of his tenure they found him to be exactly that, a martinet unbending, ever seeking the means to inflict a punishment of some kind. A.B.Ted Kelly, a young seaman who had volunteered at the age of sixteen to join the Forces, was sent aloft to the 'crow's nest' to be near stifled with smoke as K.94 turned on a zig or a zag. Another form of 'discipline' was to be ordered to the peak to tightly grasp the foc'sle guard-rail as the ship bucked up and down.

Trained Operator Ted Brazier was keeping telephone watch in the C.O's cabin, lying on the bunk with a paper-back in his hands reading or chatting to the civilians constantly passing or poking the heads in, when in stepped a dapper short man with a pointed beard and moustaches like the illustration of Captain Kuttle, and a Malacca cane. He said 'Where's the C.O's cabin?' Ted slowly raised himself saying that the man was actually in it The cane flashed and a Welsh voice roared 'I am the new C.O. get properly dressed and return to me!' Ted disappeared. There was a brief foray into northern waters and another voyage to Gibraltar and back. Sick Berth Attendant Arnold 'Doc' Fenton had come to assist the lads once under the ministration of Steward Peppin

Sub.Lt. 'Jan' Riley who came on the 10th March as Gunnery Officer found a more onerous duty when detailed by 'Dai Bando' - yes, this was the name W.J.Griffiths was to be called for evermore - on his second day at sea to draw the rum. I can do no better than quote verbatim his remarks at a Columbine reunion:

The cox'n (who was meticulous in these matters) came to the wardroom and said, 'Permission to draw rum Sir', and there was the key in the cabinet. And I took out this key and was preceded by Ridley to the Spirit Room Locker getting sicker and sicker at every step, trying hard to keep up with him. The Spirit room was on one side of the flat and on the other side was the four inch magazine, and as we got down to the Spirit room flat I saw that the door of the four inch magazine was open, and there leaning against the door making horrible sea-sick noises just like I felt was one Able Seaman Reed, and there was about two square feet of magazine deck scrubbed, and there was a pail, and there was poor A.B.Reed, and there was the Cox'n. and the Cox'n said,

'My dear fellow, what are you doing? Why Able Seaman Reed are you not scrubbing the deck of the four inch magazine?'

'Because,' said Reed, I need some fresh water Cox'n'

'Tell me' said the Cox'n, 'why do you need fresh water?'

'Well,' said Reed, because I've been sick in it.'

Then the Cox'n, with a sympathetic look on his face said,' My dear chap that's absolutely nothing. 'Why' he continued, 'only this morning have I rectified the Chief's and P.O.'s latrine with my arm up to there! So I suggest that you might press on with what you've got in your bucket.'

We opened up the Spirit Room and even when you're feeling all right the smell is ghastly, and I immediately keeled over'.

Tragedy struck on the 23rd June. It was Sub.Lt Ball's birthday, it was also the birthday of Ldg Sig Burnett and arrangements had been made for a double celebration in a local pub in Southampton where Columbine was berthed. At 'tot-time' Burnett accepted the usual 'sippers' from all messes to mark his birthday, becoming very very drunk. There were no V/S watches kept while tied along side and a 'Make and Mend' allowed the men to go early ashore. Burnett had been put in his bunk to sleep off the rum, and Brazier was to awaken the birthday lad in time to attend his party. Teatime, 1530 hrs, was too early so Ted decided to leave it until 1830 before going down to give his 'killick' a shake. The man was dead. Lying on his back suffocated by vomit.

Rushing to the phone Brazier summoned the naval hospital for an ambulance then went below to report to the Captain. He had been dhobying before his gruesome discovery and was still stripped to the waist and drying soapsuds clung to his arms when he knocked on the door and peeked round the curtain. Dai Bando was sitting there with his wife and from the drawn curtain Brazier said urgently, 'Could I see you for a moment Sir, it's important'

'Go and get yourself properly dressed signalman!' Dai yelled.

'But, Sir, you must come' -

'Go and get dressed!'

Brazier tried again, 'There's some trouble up for'ard I must report Sir, do come.'

The irate Griffiths, evidently incensed by the rating defying him in front of his wife, nearly exploded, while Ted Brazier cast all pretence of protocol aside to say bluntly,' The yeoman's lying dead in his bunk and the ambulance is on its way.'

Mrs.Griffiths screamed and Lt.Griffiths shot from the room like someone in a mighty hurry, to find the shore-based Leading S.B.A. already working on the body, having emptied half a bucket of rum out of the North Wales lad but it was to no avail, the body grew ever colder and the disgorged liquid was taken by the authorities with the result that an A.F.O - Admiralty Fleet Order - was promptly issued regarding the cessation of issuing 'neaters' in corvettes. The first instruction brought the ratio of three to one, but after a week of cooks of the mess walking past the issuing officer and Cox'n to pour the unpalatable muck over the side, a further order came with the standard enforced of two to one, two parts of water to one part rum, which was indeed required to prop up faint souls. As on the occasion when leaving Londonderry six or seven weeks later. Brazier was on watch and spotted a body in the water and reported it.

'Leave it.' Came the response from the Bridge.

Then Ted saw another body, and another and yet another. Columbine was alone, so she was stopped, a dinghy lowered and pulled toward the floating bodies too heavy to be hauled inboard by the sickened young Sub.Lt Riley so they were strung together and towed behind them, back to the waiting K94 where there was more muscle-power. The men proved to be the crew of a Canadian aircraft, one of whom was carrying a photo of his recent wedding in Glasgow. It wanting a couple of days before having to go back to 'Derry, Dai Bando conducted an official 'Burial at Sea' service, when a White 'Duster' used for the purpose unfortunately went over with the corpse to send Dai (in the words of my informant) 'back to square one.'

The very next day, A.B. Jock Bruce, an Aberdonian and a survivor from Mountbatten's **Kelly**, was on look-out duty for'ard and had stationed himself on the four inch gun platform being flattened against the gun shield by the force of the head-wind, and screwing up his eyes as protection - he later averred. The C.O. on the Bridge took a sudden notion to climb onto the front of the Bridge, grab hold of the for'ard stay and lower himself down like a monkey when, over the gun he let go to drop on to the gun-shield teetering on the edge to look down at the rating. When finally he screamed his charge, Jock almost dropped dead with fright.

At Londonderry Trained Operator Ted Brazier learned that he'd successfully passed the examination for the 'Hook' and quite naturally, as he wanted to be married proving his potential to his bride, preparatory to departure he stitched the insignias of Leading Signalman to his uniform On the way to the train he was arrested by Lt.Griffiths who accused him of being improperly dressed.

Sub.Lt. Peter Breton the OOD, who had joined Columbine earlier at Belfast, 21st March I think, and Brazier attempted to explain that the new rate had come through that day, but Dai played his ace:

'You are not <u>officially</u> a Leading Hand until you've been confirmed by me. I shall do that after your leave. Remove those badges before taking the next liberty-boat.' And he took Breton aside with the obvious intention of giving him a reprimand for allowing a rating across the gangway, 'improperly dressed'.

Once more came convoys south to Gibraltar and West Africa. One such made memorable when as 'Canteen boat' of the group Columbine went carrying messages around the convoying merchantmen. One of these, a passenger/cargo vessel, held a number of out-ward bound WAAF's who cheerfully waved and called to the men on watch and off watch as they passed. Days later the convoy ran into trouble with a U-boat pack and when at first light the list of lost ships was promulgated the men were saddened to find the ship's name carrying the girls was part of that list. Later passing through the ranks of merchant vessels they were delightfully surprised to see about four WAAF's waving like mad from another vessel astern of the one they'd originally been on, and could only assume they'd been picked up when the first ship had gone down, that they <u>were</u> in fact part of the larger unit. When <u>that</u> ship was sunk the following night the whole ship's company on K94 mourned and were downcast for weeks after.

Once again as I write, I wonder where Monsarrat found his inspiration for 'The Cruel Sea'. Glancing back through these pages I see so many instances bearing similarity to those in his novel; or did EVERY corvette ploughing the seven seas undergo such instances as that quoted above, the stopping engines in perilous waters, seamen getting blown to pieces by their own depth charges, junior officer following his C.O. to another ship, et cetera? Certainly is curious and as Alice said, it 'could get curiouser and curiouser'.

Rushing through the Bay of Biscay, abreast of Lorient, strident alarm bells brought 'action stations' and Chesty Wheeler to the Bridge. He sent McCall who had reported 'Something like an E-boat bearing down directly ahead' aft to his action station post with Telegraphist Roberts. 'Chesty' had passed for the 'hook' and had assumed temporary duty as yeoman vice the 'Discharged Deceased' Burnett who had been replaced by Ord. Sig. Irvine Stott now on his first time at sea, to make up the complement.

When Brazier's eyes adjusted to the darkness he could see, not an E-boat but a submarine and its conning tower creating a tremendous bow-wave as it submerged facing them. The American OOW, Lt. Wallis who had rung the alarm gave Dai Bando this information as he handed control to the C.O. On the foc'sle all was bustle shove and shout as the four inch gun crew closed up, loaded the gun and got ready to fire at the U-boat directly over the peak. But the Captain of the Gun, the 'Buffer', wasn't there! So when the C.O. yelled 'Fire!' down to them, A.B.Taffy Gill yelled back to say P.O.Liss was missing. W.J.Griffiths hit the roof, striding to and fro like a caged and impatient tiger as the U-boat's conning tower was rapidly disappearing. Then up came Frank Liss, clanking along the steel deck to the gun platform.

'Where is it? Where the devil is it?' he demanded fretfully.

'There, 'Buffs', shouted Gill pointing wildly over the stem, 'it's there, just there!'

The Captain of the Gun glanced in the direction of the now almost invisible enemy and then back to Ron Gill.

'No, not THAT...my tin hat' he snarled, 'some bastard's pinched my tin hat!'

Depth charge patterns were dropped but K94 was unable to claim a 'kill' and of course Frank earned a few snide remarks that released him from any charges of 'dereliction of duty'.

When they reached Gibraltar it was to find that a Group Regatta was to be held and the sloop **Enchantress** loaned Columbine a whaler in order that she might take part in the 'Young Seaman's Race'. Taking the whaler on board, all unnecessary fittings were removed including the spare oar, and the boat put alongside the **Sandwich** ready for the off. However in a power-boat tied nearby, someone noticed how low the borrowed boat was riding in the water and decided that K94 had the wrong whaler and that a swop had to be made. The Columbine lads weren't too pleased about that because they had put in a fair bit of practice and were happy with their boat. However the race began and the 'Take-over' crew were heading by two lengths halfway down the course, when they broke an oar. They were a mite disadvantaged with no replacement and 'Ping' Lee from the K94 asdic cabin and his fellow oarsmen taking the lead, won handsomely. Priced at 8 to 1 on the Tote amongst the ships in the regatta, they celebrated in the usual manner.

Back in 'Derry on the 20th October after further voyages in company with the sloops **Enchantress, Sandwich, Leith** and corvettes **Anchusa, Aubretia,** and **Violet,** they were given another boiler clean.

Meantime there had been crew changes: in addition to Bob Lee, A.B.Jim Heys joined the asdic team, P.O.Len Gilbertson on radar, Lt.Garman came as Number One, Lt.Macmanus as Signals Officer. The communications team also received the chronicler of this history Signalman 'Sabu' Wilkins. What now follows is his personal story.

Chapter 11

The lorry shuddered to a stop, the tail-board fell with a rattle, a voice called, 'Ratin' for Columbine, 'op out 'ere!.

I had arrived. Dropping with my hammock and kit-bag to the quayside, I looked at the first ship that I had ever seen at close quarters, feeling considerably intimidated at the prospect of entering a completely new world. Then a recognisable North Country shout came from the Bridge of this vessel.

'What the hell are YOU doing here?

It was Irvine Stott, a lad from Rochdale - 'Ginger' we used to call him when he occupied the bunk opposite mine in the training camp at St.Budeaux, Devonport four months previously. After 'passing out' I had been posted to a Port War Signal Station on an island in the River Forth (Inchkeith) with a recommendation for early advancement and there qualified as a Signalman. Ginger evidently, had received a draft chit to Columbine as Ordinary Signalman. His voice reached me again, and Wow! How good it felt to realise that up there was, among all **possible** strangers, a face that I knew.

'Don't forget to salute the quarterdeck when you come up the gang-way or the Cox'n'll have yer guts fer garters!'

Having been shown where my gear was to be stowed I made my way to the Bridge to report to the killick Ted Brazier whose first order to me resulted in my first and only period of 'jankers' some months into the future. He said, 'Ah, you're the replacement for McCall - I see you know 'Ginger', that could be a help, maybe. Anyway, arm yourself with a bucket, take it aft and bring back some hot water and strongers'.

I knew what a bucket was and found one, I knew aft was the other direction from the pointed end, but... strongers? I had heard of left-handed hammers, and had laughed at the apocryphal tale of the coder sent aloft with a pail and toothbrush to sweep the atmospherics off the aerial, so I was oblivious of the sub-lieutenant supervising some sort of activity on the Pom-pom platform mid-ships, until:

'SIGNALMAN!'

I went over to the officer regarding me with obvious displeasure.

'Is it not customary signalman to salute when passing an officer?'

'Sorry. . .didn't see you.'

'SIR'

'Sir, I added...rather late.

'What is your name?'

'Wilkins...er...Sir, Signalman Wilkins, just come aboard, Sir.'

'Then signalman Wilkins I would strongly recommend that you keep your eye on me because I shall certainly be watching you.'

Once aft a kindly stoker, possibly Les Harding, told me where I could obtain the hot water, and that a hand-full of soda would transform it to 'strongers' With the steaming solution in my hand I made a studied salute as I went back to the Bridge, my task . . .to clean the canvas and woodwork.

At 'Stand-easy' I went below to my Mess in the foc'sle, Mess Six, the Communications Mess. Next for'ard was the Stokers, opposite, the Seamen, and asdics/radar. Behind my Mess was the bath-room equipped with three wash basins and a kind of tray about a yard and a half square, ten or so inches high, with a nozzle in the deck-head above it. This served as a shower, and a dhoby centre. Against the bulkhead was a hot water cylinder frequented by half a million cockroaches. Ginger and the other Ord. Sig making up our trio, Tod Staniforth (another North Country chap but from Yorkshire) told me to squat on the bench at our table lining the bulkhead while tea was brewed, then Tod reached for the sugar stored in a shallow cup-board above and behind me. It was brown sugar and it was contained in an emptied five-pound biscuit tin.

'How many?' he asked.

'One heaped' I replied then watched aghast as he nonchalantly scooped a cock-roach from the tin's interior, squashed it between his fingers and threw it into the 'gash' bin, grinning 'One down, ten billion to go.' The same imperturbable behaviour was exhibited when he grasped the tin of milk having two holes punctured in the top and blew into one of these holes to release the cockroach entrapped in the other. The tea was strong, sweet, and had no discernable sign of contamination.

Having no shore going 'oppo' as yet I stayed onboard when the liberty-men went into Derry and wrote home.

Dear Mum, I'm not allowed to tell you where I am, but I can tell you I've joined a ship called Columbine and it'll be our job to guard our merchant sailors and sink U-boats if possible. It's a very small ship Mum, but I think I'll like it better than a pusser cruiser or battle-ship. I've met on board a chap who was in training with me at the Impregnable but in the other class and he comes from a Lancashire town called Rochdale but I don't

Ted Brazier ... Now a 'Leading Signalman'

think he knows Gracie Fields all that well. My Leading Hand is a Londoner, Harringay I think, or round about, north of the Thames anyway, and you would like him I think. To me he seems to know his job and gives out like he's pretty efficient, yet I would guess he's only two or maybe three years older than me. He'll definitely have his hands full with a bunch of OD's like us. I'll get this posted before we sail tomorrow.

We sailed out of Londonderry and out to the open sea to exercise guns and asdics, coming back to Moville to moor on a night of squalls, the rain laden clouds obliterating moon and stars; but cradled within that shelter I somehow regained the stomach that had been displaced by my first losing argument with sea-sickness.

Twice more I endured this torment, and then on the 5th November a slight commotion on the jetty at Moville signalled the end of Dai Bando's term on board K94 when Lieutenant John Grose RNR walked up the gangway as the hardliner W.J.Griffiths walked down. No ceremony, no cheering, in fact I saw relief registered on every face as crewmen watched the sudden replacement at 18.30 hrs when as soon as possible afterwards we slipped to make all possible haste to rendezvous with the **Enchantress** waiting at the mouth of the Foyle, the new Commanding Officer coming to the Bridge at 22.30hrs.

As we sailed ever southward so I lost my sea-sickness to find sea legs that I would never lose from then on. I watched fascinated by porpoises performing aquatic variations around the bows of **Enchantress** on our Port quarter, I stood at the Port signal lamp hypnotised by the flash of flying fish skimming the foam-flecked wavelets, and soaring over colourful islands of Portuguese-men-of-War making colonies as they creamed past Columbine's flank. We covered 1826 miles at 13 knots, expending 40 per cent of our fuel to arrive at Gibraltar on the 15th November.

We left on the 17th, picked up a convoy and took it to Freetown. On the way, off Casablanca, the smoke twenty-five miles away of a small French liner (not the Eridon) was spotted and K94 was, as usual, ordered to intercept and vet. A great deal of frustrated desire gripped the Jolly Jack Tars in Columbine on drawing nearer to the Frenchman when they clapped eyes on the waving female passengers lining the rails wearing practicably no clothes and the briefest of shorts. French or English, language is no bar in these situations and even Peter Ridley was incited to voice his appreciation with the one word, 'Lush', followed by a queer growling sound in his throat.

Identity established, procedure satisfied, the mademoiselles now possibly au fait with a few ambiguous bits of English vernacular, Columbine returned on station

Although Sub.Lt. Ball, a qualified medic prior to his volunteering to serve in the navy, advised everyone to go easy exposing oneself to the sun as we moved south, it came as no surprise to get a signal in Freetown commanding all ships to take part in a flag exercise. So there we were, Tod, Ginger, and me, with Ted Brazier ensuring that we had the bunting the right way up, rushing from flag locker to halyard, the sweat eased from our pores by the imbibed afternoon 'tot'. Senior officers had set the pace, but luckily no lower deck rating collapsed and at last, when the last flag fluttered to the chocks at the yard-arm, some kind soul below sent up a stone jar of lime juice to the Bridge. Never was a dose of 'limers' more welcome. When my skin took on a dark pigmentation instead of a rosy hue, my shipmates began to address me as 'Sabu', or 'Sab' for short, after the young actor who had achieved fame in the film 'Gunga Din'. Lieutenant Grose also acquired a nick-name that he wasn't then aware of, Slim Jim'.

There were a couple of runs ashore. Then on the Bridge one day I signalled the depot ship Philoctetes our readiness to proceed, took a convoy north to Gibraltar and there breasted to take on oil at the vessel moored to a buoy mid-harbour. Hoses spread across our deck to the **Aubretia** tied alongside, Slim repaired

Lumley Beach

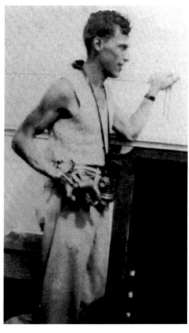

Sub. Lt. Peter Breton

Sub. Lt. Michael Ball

Back Row (L-R) Roberts, Davies, Staniforth

Centre Row (L-R) Coltar, Smith, Butcher, Stott, Me

Front Row (L-R) Davis, MacManus, Brazier, Eamer

on board **Aubretia** for a brief parley, returning when oiling of both ships was done. **Aubretia** slipped; five minutes later Columbine too slipped following the wake of her sister ship to the destroyer pens. A sudden impulse gripped Slim Jim when his ship turned slowly to Starboard and he called an order to the engine room, held aloft a handkerchief calling 'Good-bye, Goodbye' as we flashed past overtaking the astonished crew of **Aubretia** to bend the stern of a vessel tied up on the Mole. I have no way of telling what explanation was made to Capt. 'D' the next morning, I merely received the signal urging attendance.

From December to June 1944 we were on convoy duties between Gibraltar and Freetown with the odd diversions to Casablanca, Lagos, Accra and Dakar, the last notable for a huge mountain of ground-nuts on the jetty which were indicative of a future diet of peanut butter, peanut bread, peanut beer even; in fact peanut everything

At Freetown a chance meeting with an old Admiralty buddy led Macmanus to a party and dance at an establishment in the hills above the town. Like Cinderella he left at mid-night to catch the last liberty boat to find it holding a bevy of 'four-ringers' and commanders, and a boat's cox'swain who was totally bewildered in the fog-filled river and unable to locate Columbine on her buoy, put our signals officer on the first ship that he could see . . . **the Enchantress**. Mac was to stay the night, Grose and Garman on K94 grew concerned, Signalman Stott overhearing the Number One say, 'Where the blazes can he have got to? Ought to be back by now. I think he might've fallen in the 'oggin', and the skipper's mumbling under-tone, 'I shall be very offended Garman if he is drowned'.

Lt. Garman received word when we got back to Gibraltar that his wife in England was seriously ill, and applied for compassionate leave which was readily granted, his position as First Lieutenant then assumed by the Signals Officer Lt. Macmanus who took all the Communications Branch, signalmen, telegraphists and coders, to a classy joint ashore for tea and cakes then to a photographers for a group photo which they all signed.

The 13th July, it was yet another thirteen, we were given orders by Capt 'D' Gib. to patrol the Strait to prevent the access of U-boats into the Mediterranean. Up and down we went between Algecirus and Ceuta carefully avoiding the restricted areas within the three-mile limit of territorial waters.

I took over the afternoon Watch in a thick mist, look-outs on either side of the Bridge, aft by the D.C's, mid-ships on the boat-deck, one man on the foc'sle. Gliding wraith-like at six knots through the white blanket, apprehensive in the extreme that at any moment in the crossing of the sea-lane we might penetrate either an incoming or outgoing convoy, all eyes were skinned for the sight of anything more tangible than a rain cloud. A sudden gust disturbed the airy mantle and I saw the signal lamp of the trawler patrolling nearest to the 'Rock' winking at us. Black Swan told us she had made an asdic contact she thought was a U-boat. I reported this to the OOW who called down to Slim in his cabin who came bounding up to the Bridge in seconds to have a message sent to Capt 'D' for support. The SDO Jim Heys reported a 'ping' a definite contact that galvanised instant activity as the ship's company went to Action Stations.

Subby Breton switched on the amplifier so that all Bridge personnel could hear the ping, ping, ping.

'Moving left Sir'. The steady voice of Jim Heys came through the opened hatch of the asdic cabin.

Grose gave an order to the waiting Ridley on the wheel, the echo merged into an almost continuous sound as K94 reached her top speed of sixteen knots and the firing button released the depth charges. Gigantic spouts of water erupted from a placid sea.

'Hard to Port' murmured Grose and we swung round with canted deck in a narrow sweep, our eyes glued to where the cascading sea was returning to its element. Silence. Nothing. I watched the spiralling shock-waves of the last explosion skimming over the sullen flat surface of the sea to mingle with the misty horizon, the fog coming back to crowd our endeavours.

It seemed incredible that the enemy could have escaped destruction by the tons of explosives unleashed upon her. If the contact <u>was</u> a U-boat.

The tension began to loosen but Grose had other ideas, mumbling, 'Steer one three oh', and to the asdic operators, 'Continue Searching', so the situation was now one of eerie stillness as we stood wordless on the Bridge scarcely even looking at one another, each buried in our own thoughts while searching with binoculars and telescope When once again came the repetitive ping, once again we bore down at speed to let go another batch of D.C's now ready-primed. Again witnessing the turbulence, the mountains of water, the shock of the transmitted explosions; but this time witnessing floating debris and oil. The echo had gone by the time the destroyer sent out from Gibraltar reached our position, but because we couldn't be certain of a positive 'kill' we made manoeuvres for the rest of the day through to the 'First Watch' but without making further contact. Whether the enemy went to the bottom or actually eluded our attack I shall never know, but that night watch was cold and scary, and never more efficiently kept.

Coming out from Casablanca five days after this, we ran, or <u>almost</u> ran, into a line of American Liberty boats about to enter. We were both in the swept channel, heading toward each other on collision course at a combined speed of twenty knots. On the 'Monkey Island' was Michael Ball in the small chart caboose, starboard side for'ard, disconnected from the asdic cabin by a slight wooden bulkhead. 'Slim Jim' had spent

... It seemed incredible that the enemy could have escaped destruction ...

time ashore with his pal from Aubretia and was draped over the compass with his mind some other place, at his side stood Lt. Macmanus, hands clasped behind, waiting for some movement from his commanding officer. I was fastened to the Port signal projector in sheer horror as I saw these damn great welded jobs getting closer and closer. If any officer on Columbine could lay claim to being a gentleman and an officer rather than an officer and gentleman, it was 'Mac'. I wondered if I really was out on a limb as I heard 'Mac' clear his throat in order to get a response . . .'Hmn . . . Hmn'.

'Crikey!' I thought, 'we're going to smash into the bloody things!

The hesitant noises floated over to me again and I was hopping about trying to make up my mind whether to streak over to the starboard side of the Bridge or hop it down the companionway when (it must've been a sixth sense or something) Sub. Lt. Ball came from the caboose, saw the oncoming line of ships within a cannon-ball's throw, and hurled himself at the voice-pipe yelling ' Hard a starboard!' knocking 'Slim' from the binnacle at the same time as Columbine heeled over beneath, I was convinced, were the davits of the first in line.

Yes, the Number One was a gentleman who could not dispute a point with a superior officer. He also possessed a quirky sense of humour I once caught glimpse of when the gun's crew were closed up for a practice shoot. 'Mac' was on the Bridge chatting with the Gunnery Officer when the buffer, Captain of the Gun cupped his hands and bellowed up to Riley, 'Gun's cocked Sir!'

The First Lieutenant glanced at Jim and said softly' 'Oh dear, will it take long to rectify the matter do you think?'

The smouldering conflict of personalities between S/Lt Jim Riley and myself came to a head after the next convoy from Freetown. As soon as Columbine and the other escorts had completed the job of oiling and berthing I received an R.P.C. for this officer and took it down to the Ward-room to inform him that a sister ship (I forget which) Requested the Pleasure of his Company at 1900 hours that evening. I then went to the Wireless Caboose where I borrowed a set of head-phones to tune to the local radio station on the secondary receiver. Do not remember how long I was there listening but I do recall starting to feel that time was pressing and that about mid-way through a performance of The *Dance of Death* by Saint-Saens I was gripped by a spooky apprehension little to do with the music. Lifting the 'phones from my ears, I heard, above all else, the sound of the bosun's pipe, carrying the awful fact that as Duty Signalman I ought to have been with that rating and that officer for the harbour routine of lowering the ensign at Sunset!

Rushing topside I slithered to a halt for there was the OOD standing at the salute. I was late! Of course it HAD to be Riley in the act of performing his last duty of the day, and anticipating a fine outcome for his RPC was a picture of spotless elegance in white shirt, white shorts, white stockings, shoes, and a cap.

Quartermaster Thrift having satisfactorily carried out his part was observing the routine with interest . . . as a rule unemotional, our officer mouthed unrepeatable nautical expressions intended to expedite my lowering of the flag, but I was nervous and my fingers slipped causing me to prematurely release the halyard from its cleat. Down fluttered the sooty ensign from its eight day flight abaft the funnel to wrap itself around the head and shoulders of the fuming officer and the more he pulled and tugged the blacker he and his clothing became, all this accompanied by imprecations muffled by the flag but still unmistakable:

'I've waited a long time for this, I've got you now Wilkins, and I guarantee you Number One's!'

I saw a slow smile appear momentarily on the face of George

Thrift and then disappear. So I guessed I was relatively safe and the ten days No11's eventually awarded were stoically endured because the stoppage of shore-leave coincided with days spent at sea. It was during this time that a new esprit de corps was forged between the two of us and ended with a personal sad loss for me when Jim died after the war.

After my punishment I was sitting next to a chap in the Forces cinema in Gibraltar when he asked me what ship I served in, and on telling him 'Columbine' he said, 'Blimey mate, were there many survivors? You would've been lucky up there on the bridge wouldn't you?'

'What the hell you on about' I replied, 'I'm not a survivor. my ships' not been sunk - not to my knowledge anyhow'.

Just before Goofy got up to his usual larks my companion settled back in his seat with the remark, 'Well I call that very odd, I've definitely heard about Columbine, recognised the name as soon as you said it, got torpedoed off Freetown or Dakar or thereabouts. Must be another Columbine I guess. There's two Arabises aren't there?'

Goofy let out a howl followed by whoops from the matelots.

MINUTE OF EVIDENCE TAKEN AT ENQUIRY HELD IN THE BOARD
ROOM, COLONIAL ORPHAN CHAMBER BUILDINGS, PARLIAMENT
STREET, CAPE TOWN, on the 6th July,1944, before
MR. ALLAN SPENCER WHITE DEPUTY SHIPPING MASTER of
CAPE TOWN.

A F F I D A V I T

I, the undersigned, CHRISTIAN ALFRED HANCHE, make oath and
say :-

1. THAT I am the Chief Officer of the steamship "COLUMBINE."

2. THAT on the 9th of June, 1944, the ship left Loanda bound on
a voyage with its next port of call at Cape Town.

3. THAT on the 16th June,1944, I went on watch at 4 o'clock in
the afternoon. At or about 8 p.m. I had just taken the ship's
position and was recording in the chart room. My watch had just
finished and I was being relieved by the Third Mate, B. DAVIES.
There was a heavy swell at the time and a moderate sea. A fresh
wind was blowing.

4. THAT a loud explosion occurred on the port side just abaft
the engine room. It seemed obvious that the ship had been struck
by a torpedo. The Captain ANRE REIDAR SIMENSEN was on the bridge
at the time. He blew five blasts on the ship's whistle. This is
the signal to man the lifeboat stations. I went at once to
my boat which is of course the Chief Officer's boat, No. 4 boat on
the port side. The crew assembled at the boat stations and my
boat was successfully lowered. My boat pulled away from the ship
and shortly afterwards we heard a further explosion which we
assumed was a second torpedo striking the ship. About two minutes
later which was about ten minutes after the first explosion the
ship settled and sank. After the ship had sunk I saw the Second
Mate's boat floating near mine. I did not see the Master again after
he had blown the five whistles. My boat was picked up later by a
naval craft. None of the persons in my boat lost their lives.

5. THAT there were sixteen people in my boat.

6. THAT I attach to my Affidavit a list showing the names of all
persons on board immediately prior to the torpedo-ing.

7. THAT the "COLUMBINE" had four lifeboats only. At the time
the ship was torpedoed its position was about twenty-five miles
N.W.N. of Cape Columbine. At the time of the sinking of the ship
a fresh wind was blowing from the shore out to sea. It would not
have been possible for any person to have gained the shore except
in the lifeboats of the ship, nor would it have been possible in
that sea and wind for any person to have survived until the next
day by hanging on to wreckage.
The Master and the Third Officer and eighteen of the crew were
killed out of a crew of fifty including four naval ratings (gunners).
The ship also carried two passengers.

(Sgd).

SWORN to at CAPE TOWN this the 6th day of JULY, 1944, by the
Deponent who has acknowledged that he knows and understands
the contents of this Affidavit.

Before me,

(Sgd.)

DEPUTY SHIPPING MASTER AND
COMMISSIONER OF OATHS.

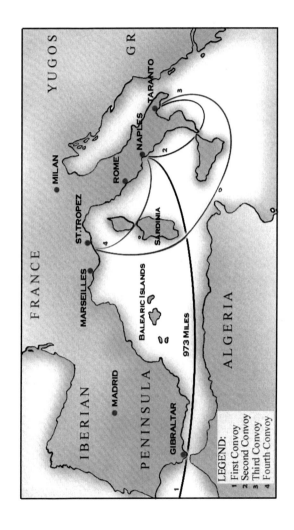

Chapter 12

Plans in high places had been going on to invade the South of France, and to this end Columbine and **Aubretia** were ordered on the 31st July to escort a large Headquarters merchant vessel to Naples where the Premier Winston Churchill was kicking his heels. Less than twenty-four hours after getting there we left for Taranto and arriving three days later made ready for 'Operation Dragoon' finding that in a fighting unit of British, American, French, and Greek vessels, we were the only corvettes with this seven and a half knot 'Delta Force Support' convoy.

On the 11th August 1944 there was hustle and bustle all over the harbour, in the town laid out in the plans of a British naval architect citizens prepared for the working day, many coming to the jetties to watch our departure; Macmanus bent to the voice-pipe.

'Ready to sail Sir', and up came the C.O. to call to S/Lt Riley and the Buffer on the foc'sle. 'Heave in'. Two minutes elapse and Jan Riley calls, 'Up and down Sir; coming home'. The captain leans toward the wheel-house voice pipe saying to the presumed cox'n, 'Slow ahead, Starboard twenty'.

No response from Ridley - the Number One had forgotten to have 'Hands to Stations' piped! As dear Mac said to me later, 'Was my face red!!'

The secret reports in the Confidential Book Room disclosed the number of men Germany had deployed in the South of France, the type and amount of training received, the gun emplacement, and even the probable state of the weather on specific dates. That British spies had been accurate in their assessment was realised on arrival at the beach-head when the most we encountered was sporadic rifle fire and the sight of disconsolate prisoners squatting on the sand. A 'Hands to bathe' was piped during which these prisoners were loaded on board waiting landing-craft to be escorted to Naples. Coming from his swim asdic rating 'Gilly Gilchrist, the K94's postman, felt a sudden excruciating pain and went down to the S.B.A. and Fenton at first glance immediately sent for the Navigator who confirmed his diagnosis. A signal was flashed to the nearest American destroyer and while two ratings sat upon the unfortunate 'Gilly', Michael Ball did what was necessary by receiving instruction by radio telephone. Our shipmate recovered - after a while. We also observed **H.M.S.Kimberley** hove to, giving temporary accommodation to Winston Churchill.

When I took over the 'Morning' from Staniforth, he whispered, 'There's hell to pay. Radar's lost t'bloody convoy. Nowt else to report - Kye in the asdic caboose. Good-night.'

At four a.m. we were enjoying a calm sea, the sky lightening from black to purple while questions and unsatisfactory answers passed between Bridge and radar tower to end with a very worried OOW calling the captain to the Bridge. Grose mounted the ladder two steps at a time scarcely noticing me, moaning in a kind of helpless exasperation, 'Why are these things always happening to me - I am surrounded with incompetence!'

'Keep your eyes skinned!' he cried to the lookouts and to me. 'I want you to report everything you see. Do you understand? Everything . . . even if it's only floating rubbish.'

Ginger Stott relieved me, Staniforth relieved him, and because we were in three watches of course, I took over the 'first dog' and at 1610 hrs saw a blob on the horizon resolve itself into the shape of a funnel. Then came another, and another when with a jubilant cry I reported the sighting. Grose acknowledged this intelligence with his usual grunt as he ordered a slight alteration in our course and probably making up his mind what he would say to the Yankee C.O. Time passed.

We came to Naples; the destroyer leading, we the 'repeating ship' next in line to copy all flags exhibited by the American to our sister **Aubretia** astern of us. When Ischia loomed to port and Capri came up on our starboard, the S.O. let loose a stream of Yankee bunting. We had these in a special locker but had only a basic idea of their import. Brazier balanced his telescope on a signal projector and as the flags left the destroyers deck called out, 'Flot-Turn-Three-Zero-Speed-One-Two. That's it, get em up!'

Stott was bending on the 'heads' I the 'tacks', Staniforth held the halyard and when I THOUGHT that I had secured the shackle of the last tack-line I hissed,' Hoist away!' and nearly died! There above my head the signal, unattached to the clip I was still holding, floated in the summer breeze like a line of dhobying.

Slim for once lost his peculiar sleepy attitude when he resorted to a particularly expressive lower deck noun, what one might truthfully describe as an improper noun.

'What blankety blank fool did that? Aren't we in enough trouble as it is? Someone get the damn thing down, and quickly.'

Brazier sort of grinned at me and said,' You'd better get up there chum, if you tell him you've volunteered to climb up to the yards to fetch it down you might get off lightly, O.K?'

Ascending the three steps from the flag lockers to the 'monkey island' I stood before Slim and saluted.

'Well, signalman?'

'I'm the er . . . blankety blank Sir'

A brief pause while he contemplated me sourly then, 'Put yourself in the First Lieutenant's report,' he growled leaving me to move a yard or two and carry out this order. Mac subsequently let me off with a reprimand and a conspiratorial frown. This was in Naples where we found another signal exercise about to erupt but in less discomfort than the battle against weather conditions at Freetown; also, this one was aimed at all ships under the command of the cruiser **Orion**, including the **Ajax**, and 'all ships wishing to take part'.

Ted Brazier waxed enthusiastic, saying it might impress Slim and that if we agreed to work the halyard he'd have a go at answering the questions. At the end of three quarters of an hour we saw our number K94 flying on the yard of H.M.S **Orion** - a complimentary signal which somewhat modified Slim's attitude toward us and we were invited to his cabin for a drink, beer, ice-cold from the fridge.

Leaving Naples where I had gone a couple of times ashore to the San Carlo Opera House to reserve tickets for the officers and myself, in company with an American destroyer but not with the Aubretia this occasion we headed for the South of France landings once more, this time through the Strait of Bonifacio that separates Corsica from Sardinia. Coming through the strait the destroyer with its faster speed made it an effort to maintain station on her when we were hit by a blustering storm. I was on the Bridge when I saw two 'Killicks' on the upper deck, one of whom I didn't recognise and was told by Lt. Breton (on watch with me) that it was Leading Seaman Pritchard who had that day been given permission to shave off his 'set', the other man being Leading Seaman Harry Prosser. Brazier had come to the Bridge and he told us that water had been seeping past the rim of the hatch on the foc'sle to wash down into the mess-decks and that the pair although 'off watch' had of their own accord come to fix the trouble with rope. Then as we were watching, an excessive bucketing of the bow brought sea water between the steel plating of the foc'sle and the semtex laid in Argentia causing it to lift, fold, and topple overboard, carrying Pritchard with it. Prosser managed to grab a guardrail stanchion holding on for dear life suffering only superficial cuts to his face and a bruise or two elsewhere.

'Man overboard!' he managed to yell, I heard it above the shrieking wind and I banged the 'Church' pennant up to the chocks on the starboard yard-arm to indicate that it was the side where our mate had gone. Brazier sent a message by light to the Yank who permitted us to stop and search, a search that continued for fully three quarters of an hour, but, in that sea and in that wind, we knew in our hearts from the outset that it would be hopeless. So, we crammed on the best speed we could to catch up with the convoy and en route as the weather abated, down below in the mess-deck Seaman Taff Edwards began the design and the construction of wreaths made of rope, emblems of death on the high seas scattered with prayers on longitude and latitude making our final passage of the Strait back to Naples two weeks later.

We were returned to the U.K. when past experience massaged our beam of 33½ feet into the Albert Dock from where short leave was granted to both watches. On their return we were berthed in the Gladstone Dock where the personal effects of our lost shipmate were auctioned for cash to be sent to his mother. I paid £1 for a toothbrush never to be used - and never did the money, <u>any</u> of the money raised by the crew, reach Mrs. Pritchard, although deducted from the pay of those contributing. This was only revealed years after the war when the <u>need too</u> had long gone. But in 1944 we were motivated by compassion and honour with no reason to doubt the action of a naval pay-bob.

The second week in November saw us steaming north on a magnificent scenic course through the Western Isles, and as the westering sun slid behind Skye to flash a last light on the

'Leading Seaman' Harold Pritchard

... Scattered with prayers ...

Isle of Rona against the Torridonian landscape on our starboard beam, Ted Brazier turned to me and said, 'Just look at that, Ted, it's really beautiful isn't it? If Fran and I have a daughter I shall call her Rona'.

On a personal note I can say that he did, and that she is indeed beautiful.

The next morning we got blown about in the Minches when a merchantman, the **Empire Trader**, requested assistance and we were able to tow her into the calmer waters of Loch Ewe before getting on our way through the Pentland Firth, and thence to a 'dicky' re-fit in Hull. One of the smaller dry-docks normally used by the fishing fleet accommodated us for a couple of weeks

Lt.Macmanus had left us in Liverpool when ordered to take passage to Ottawa to become First Lieutenant of LST 3509. In his stead came Lt. 'The admirable' Crichton, and with him came the new asdics officer Lt Evershed. He, Evershed, while waiting for K94 to arrive had spent a great deal of time in the Liverpool Stadium and had become perhaps a little too enthusiastic in the art? Sport? Comedy? of wrestling. So much so in fact that I was continually surprised by a half-nelson or some such grip, when he would creep up on me from behind when I was on watch rather like a present-day Burt Kwok in a present-day Peter Sellars film.

The return passage to our base in Liverpool was without incident except for, as I've noted, the attacks made on me by Lt. Evershed, and another glimpse of lovely Rona.

We were back in Liverpool by November 27th when orders came for Columbine to take a west-bound convoy, bound for the United States of America, a prospect that pleased me no end because for years I had entertained wild notions about cowboys and gangsters and had listened with much interest to the lads in K94 yarning about their last time over there. Alas, I never did make it.

Two days out, the 2nd December, reduced to four knots we faced a stiff wind that buffeted my face and threatened to tear away my duffel coat and oilskins. Hailstones materialised from the darkening sky all around and ahead I saw a fearsome Atlantic roller gather extra speed and proportion to reach what I estimated to be a height of forty feet. It was elemental, awesome, so as the adrenalin pumped jerkily through my veins I stood unable to move, transfixed by intense fear, wedged between the port signal projector and the port guard-rail, both hands numbed by the instinctive grip on stand and rail. A rapid glance over the flag locker behind me showed a deserted boat-deck, the port waist foaming as the seas washed down and hissed through the scuppers. The depth charges looked dreadfully unstable and angled dangerously. I watched and saw the stern rise and then fall, appearing to slide slowly in my direction. Tearing my eyes from this hallucination I turned to see another world embracing wave reaching toward me, and there was nothing I could do about it; nothing except to wait with the terrifying thought that it wanted but a few seconds before I would of a certain be swept over the side to eternity. For a brief, the briefest of moments I saw Columbine's bows attempt to climb the monster ahead of her, but there came a sickening lurch, a mighty crunch as she came to momentary stop and down poured the mountainous wave. Down it came, tearing away the forepart of the Bridge, scraping the front of the asdic cabin over the side to expose the startled and scared Jim Heys suspended on a bulk-head hook by his clothes. It swamped the 'monkey island', it swamped me, as it swirled and eddied at my feet then shot down the ladder to the wheel-house. Lt.Ball had been catapulted from the little chart caboose still holding on to a drawer that had come free of the chest, destroying the uprights of the caboose in taking Mike to the back of the Bridge, but I was unhurt and due to oil-skins, duffel coat, sow'ester and sea-boots, completely dry! I watched him go below to shift into another rig then heard a faint voice coming from a pipe: 'Wheel-house - Fore bridge'.

Ted Brazier with a cold chisel and a hammer was busy trying to move the distorted top of the asdic caboose to give Heys freeway so I loosened my grip on the rail to stagger across and up the three steps to the voice pipe, and lifted the cover.

'Bridge - Wheel-house'.

'Leading Telegraphist Davis on the wheel Sir, Quartermaster Thrift was knocked unconscious when he was hit by flying glass and is feeling groggy and needs some attention. What course shall I steer Sir?'

Well. I looked around the Bridge; there was no one except me and Ted. I gave him the message from Dai Davis and cannot now remember who turned us or how, but turn we did. What remains in the memory is Grose suggesting that I go aloft with an Aldis lamp! Not only had the wave hurt the man on the wheel, it had flooded the wireless office behind the wheel-house to render the apparatus within completely inoperative.

Although we now had a stern sea, we were still steaming in a state of isolation caused by the elements; riding on a crest we saw little of the other ships as they wallowed in the troughs, and when we were down we became invisible to them, and in that tight corner, no way was I going to attempt anything as foolhardy, and Slim accepted my refusal, deciding there was no alternative and that we must return to Londonerry or Liverpool without a signal of any kind to the S.O.Escort. As a fighting unit we were helpless, the impact of the wave had opened the foc'sle hatch and partially flooded the mess deck, spilled down the funnel to slop around the boiler room, created superficial damage all over the vessel. With the radio out of action, the asdics wrecked, and the four-inch gun having elevating and training gears jammed by distortion, shield buckled and platform shield flattened out, it was time to go home. Lt.Grose ordered an extra issue of rum to be made - neat.

The next morning when reporting to the Bridge I was told that Columbine had survived yet another danger. During the night an

aircraft of Coastal Command had made a run at us with bomb doors open, but luckily our recognition signal made with the Aldis by 'Ginger' was translated as being correct and the blighter sheered off.
Evidently we had been spotted in a position no ship ought to have been, and the pilot would then have radioed this information to prevent a possible mistake later.

We got back to Liverpool on the 4th December and

Asdics wrecked, 4 inch gun out of action

squeezed our thirty-three feet plus five and a half inches through the Salthouse Half-tide into the Albert Dock where we were to remain until 20th March 1945 undergoing an almost complete overhaul.

Bob Lee left, Dai Davis left (on a C.W.Course), Peter Breton and Jan Riley were made up to full lieutenants.

We sailed in the early morning of Tuesday 19th April; a quiet still morning full of lower deck 'buzzes' mainly wildly improbable until putting in at Moville on the Foyle. We could not get away from the jetty the next afternoon. Three times Columbine moved a yard or two then was shoved back by the blustering wind. Then a parcel of press-ganged land-lubbers braced themselves against the wall and the combined muscle-power applied with poles and boathooks sent us on our way; all going well until a couple of miles down stream we ran onto the dreaded mud-flats, wrecked our asdic dome and had to call out two tugs to get us afloat and capable of making Liverpool for repair. We missed the convoy of course.

Three weeks later we took on a bundle of boffins with their balloons to sail the northern waters off Ireland weather reporting in the hope of gaining reliable information to help the allied armies on the impending invasion of Normandy. Steaming at a lazy three knots on a gentle sea. I had the 'second dog', it was a quiet evening, a quiet time for reflecting on one's past and future. Alone on the wide wide sea with a blue sky and dolphins as playmates. The peace overtaking my spirits completely when news came on the wireless that the German armies in Italy had surrendered on the 2nd May. We spliced the 'Main brace'; and did so again six days later on the capitulation of the entire armies and navy of The Third Reich.

The 15th May we left Albert Dock for the last time, taking the last convoy to Gibraltar and on our arrival I celebrated by walking from the docks along Main Street and turning left just past the British Bobby on traffic duty always there, to hear a wonderful performance of Handels 'Messiah' in the Cathedral of the Holy Trinity by the army personnel stationed on the 'Rock'. We left Gibraltar on the 30th May in company with one of the newer corvettes, the **Oakham Castle**, and the submarine **Spirit**. Steaming through the Bay of Biscay with the sea moderate and the air still. I was looking over the side of Columbine's Bridge thinking that I would probably never again see a porpoise or a flying fish when above the throb of our engine I could hear the sound of a mouth-organ coming from the boat-deck and when my watch was finished I went to see what it was all about. There was the harmonica player lugubriously intoning 'Let The World Go By' and something to do

HMS Oakham Castle

BUILT by A & J Inglis of Glasgow and completed in 1944, she then joined the Liverpool Escort Pool, part of the Western Approaches Command, and engaged on Gibraltar convoy escort duties until May 1945.

On May 30 with HMS Columbine she escorted the submarine HMS Spirit to Portsmouth and on completion of this duty returned to Liverpool.

In June 1945 she was loaned to Rosyth being employed on training duties. Then followed long periods in dockyard hands for modification, repairs and refits lasting until 1950 at Clyde, Devonport, Portland and Portsmouth.

During December 1950 she was reduced to reserve at Plymouth. She remained in reserve until July 1957 when she was transferred to the Air Ministry for conversion to an ocean weather ship.

The conversion carried out by James Lamont, Port Glasgow was completed on April 3, 1958 and she was renamed Weather Reporter on May 16, 1958.

S. 132

(G.V.(b) W.L. 1026/D7619. 5000 Pads. 7/45. B. & S. Ltd. Gp. 915.

NAVAL MESSAGE.

For use in Signal Department only	*The last message recieved at sea by H.M.S Columbine. 2nd June 1945.*		
Originators Instructions (Indicate of Priority Intercept Group, etc.)		Codress/Plaindress	No. of Groups
TO: *Columbine*		FROM: *O. Castle*	

We of Oakham Castle would record our appreciation of having made the last operational trip in company with Columbine. May the achievements of Columbine during these past grim days be a source of inspiration to each and every one of you during the difficult days to come. We wish you Good speed and safe voyages.

1851

System	P/L Code or Cypher	Receip.	Despatch	Operator	P.O.O.W.	Date
TBS						2/6/45

with 'Galway' - all-round him were gathered the maudlin matelots conducted by A.B.Stanley wielding a huge carving knife as a baton.

A.B.'Boyo' Rees brought the show to a stop when, after singing a catchy melody - but in Welsh - he invited everybody to 'Join in the Chorus!' Each side of the yard-arm perched a sparrow named by Lt.Evershed, 'Peabody' and 'Building'. They stopped singing too.

Columbine as a Royal Navy stop-gap was out of a job. 'She had fought and dealt with the human and elemental angers, she had sheltered me as I grew to manhood recognising my own strengths and weakness, given me the bonding and comradeship of a great company of Englishmen. I was going to miss them all with my next draft chit, particularly those of Mess Six: Brazier, Eric Davis, T.C.Smith, Roberts, Coltart, Eamer, Butcher, Stott and Staniforth, Sollieux and Knox. We shook hands and parted at Faslane on the Garelock on the 16th June 1945.

A skeleton crew ferried her over to Lock Foyle where she lay for four years until the Admiralty sold her to Anders Jahre of Sandefjord for use as a whale tow-boat and after, a whale catcher named **Leif Welding**. which was sold for scrap in 1966. Sic Gloria.

The new owners boxed her original name-board and magnanimously sent it to Ted Brazier to be put on show at future re-unions.

Chapter 13

It was during the refit forced on Columbine after 'The Wave' that an invitation to a 'Coming of Age Party' arrived on board from an old salt who had whilst serving in the dreadnought H.M.S. Albion watched soldiers expiring in oceans of blood ripped from their flesh by submerged barbed wire at Gallipoli in 1915. Called back to the Service in middle age at the commencement of war in 1939 he had first been involved in anti-contraband duties in the eastern Mediterranean from where he was semi-invalided to Plymouth when he applied for a transfer to Liverpool. Scouse had come home, securing a post in the Signal Distribution Office at Gladstone Dock.

A week before Christmas 1944, accompanied by a dozen of my shipmates I went along to that party meeting his daughter, and in later months was wont to quote 'Othello'

'She bade me, if I had a friend that lov'd her
I should but teach him how to tell my story
And that would woo her. Upon this hint I spake:
She lov'd me for the dangers I had pass'd,
And I lov'd her that she did pity them'

My future wife and I used those five months, that oasis of peace in a country at war, discovering shared delight in music, in poetry, in the exploration of the Wirral countryside where, one golden day at a now famous beauty spot I wrote in my diary: 'It was like a dream reclining there on the Thurstaston hill over-looking the slow ripple of waves on the Dee and watching the play of sea-gulls overhead swooping and gliding, their raucous scream splitting the quiet as with mocking jest. The sun kissing the sand to make it blush into a shining amber glow, transforming clusters of stones and shells into exquisite emeralds' and so at the age of twenty-one I was visited by the love that was never to leave me.

Three months later I sat in Mess 38 in the cruiser **H.M.S.Jamaica** in Plymouth Sound inexpressively relieved that the war with Japan had ended, yet strangely perturbed by another fear - the possible further use of the terrifying inhuman device that had flattened Hiroshima with such colossal loss of life.

We sailed on the 23rd August 1945 and peace was in the air. In the sky, a lone war-plane skittered, twisted, faltered, and fell into the sea. **Jamaica** instantly lowered a boat to recover the body of a young man who might have been dreaming of a career outside of a coloured uniform. I felt sickened; the warring armies had finished the devil's work and this seemed one death too many. He was buried that afternoon with an impromptu service. Afterwards we pumped up 22 knots to reach Malta in five days during which time I made a friend in Signalman Harry Alan Lord and found the routine of four watches instead of three as in Columbine a definite improvement. Especially in regard to the extra hours of sleep I could enjoy not withstanding initial difficulty when slinging my hammock in a starboard passage outside the cabin of a sub-lieutenant doing things with a violin which would have made Menhuin or Szigetti take up the banjo in disgust.

Put ashore at St. Paul's Bay with an Aldis Lamp I took part in a night exercise, called at the Vernon Club with my new friend Harry, bought ourselves Number Six rig-outs, took snaps of each other on the rocky foreshore at Sliema to send home. Nothing else of interest worth mentioning.

The passage through Suez and The Red Sea with the cruiser H.M.S.Glasgow was uneventful except for gunnery and boat drills and a signal exercise bringing me a pat on the back from the officer conducting the quiz arranged between the two warships. Taking it in turn one ship fired a question by flashing light to the other when the Bridge personnel relayed it throughout the vessel by loudhailer. Five minutes was the allotted time to get an answer back and toward the grand finale we were lying neck and neck when Jamaica's Signal Officer turned and said to the air, 'Has anyone got a question to floor them? Get this, and we've won'.

Never volunteer they say, but somehow I found myself responding, 'Yes sir, ask 'em if they know whose first symphony was extolled as a glorious tenth by his contemporaries'.

He looked over to me and said, 'Yes, well I suppose there's nothing about not using non-naval questions in the competition. You know the answer of course signalman?'

'Of course sir... Johannes Brahms'.

In the year of 2000 I met the Chief Yeoman who had served in the cruiser H.M.S.Glasgow at that time and he remembered the occasion and that they lost the quiz to the Jamaica by one question and that the question was 'something to do with music'. I had great satisfaction in telling him that the question was mine.

But in 1945 I could still lose my way in the labyrinthine corridors and compartments below decks in my new home as I sought conversation in the S.D.O. with Ldg Telegraphist Embry, the man who had replaced Eric Davis in Columbine, while a day or two after leaving Aden a flurry of excitement took me to the Flag Deck to witness my first sighting of a torpedo launch. There was a whale surfaced ahead. It had been certified dead; not by the ship's doctor, but by the eagle-eyed Officer of the Watch who had instantly diagnosed a remedy for this hazard to shipping, and I without more ado, scuttled below to avoid the smell that followed us on the prevailing wind eastwards to Colombo, the chief port of the lovely island then called Ceylon, these days, Sri Lanca, and one time, Serendip. With others I was offered a trip in an ancient goods train to the Capital city of Kandy, rattling uncomfortably through jungle settlements and sustained with K-Rations (American devised survival kits), to see The Temple of The Tooth, a Buddhist shrine from where an exotic plant was garnered and posted to Liverpool for my Irene when Jamaica reached Trincomalee a couple of days later.

Trincomalee, one of the world's largest natural harbours, which still held a number of Navy vessels and as a consequence plenty of activity ashore for the ratings, including a rather smart establishment known as the Vernon Club. Here I enjoyed a piano recital, a brilliant E Flat Polonaise by Chopin included, as encore by a John Vallier whom regretfully I knew not and still don't. On the 10th November 45 I was playing snooker with Sig Griffiths, though it wasn't Terry I guess. Then 14 days later I stood on the flag deck as Jamaica steamed up the Irrawadi or Rangoon River open-mouthed at the ornate magnificence of the Schwe Dagon Pagoda ahead starboard side, sending scintillating shafts of tropical sun spinning off the beautifully carved spire. Covered with sheets of gold leaf we were told. We were also told that our arrival that day had averted trouble from over 50,000 natives massed at the temple protesting against British occupancy although, when I went ashore that afternoon with my oppo Harry Alan Lord, the only belligerent activity sprang from a bunch of ragamuffins clambering for cigarettes, ticklers or tailor made, as we passed two stone lions or chinthays to remove our shoes preparatory to the climb up 156 stone steps. At the top we got to a circular plateau which supports the temple building soaring skywards and we viewed some of the 64 small intricately carved teak shrines that surround the golden dome, called Tazoungs where candles burn and offerings are made to Buddha, Three or four dogs sprawled panting in the blaze of sun we noted as we left to return to the ship where we saw a party dancing the light fantastic on the quarterdeck. Officers with their partners swayed to music provided by the band of the Royal Marine Portsmouth Division. As we climbed on board port side we were subjected to a search to prevent the importation of bottled beer. This was no doubt necessary because a later incident revealed the too often revealed talent of jack tar to imbibe a shade too copiously . . . when a stoker lost his way on board to find himself in the First Lieutenant's cabin and when Commander Casement returned from conference with Captain Hughes-Hallett he WAS RATHER TAKEN ABACK TO BE OFFERED A DRINK FROM HIS OWN DECANTER. Thereafter one always referred to a particular forward mess as the stokers METH deck.

Following a brief call on Java where a run ashore at Surabaya was aided and abetted by the gift of Guilders from the Dutch Government, Jamaica turned her nose southwards and into a message from the Equator Hydro-telegraphic Station, relayed by Courier Flying Fish reading:

'My South Atlantic Porpoise Patrol reports that His Majesty's Ship Jamaica was proposing to enter my illustrious domain for the first time on the ninth day of December 1945. Queen Amphitrite and I are looking forward to your visit and my bears are delighted to hear of such a large number of novices. We shall arrive on board at 0945 on the 9th day of December with a fanfare of trumpets, roars of bears, and members of my

court for the ceremony of initiation in accordance with ancient custom. Please make adequate preparation... signed, His Maritime Majesty King Neptune, by Grace of Mythology Lord of All the Waters and Sovereign of All Oceans'

We crossed the 'Line' close to Addu Atoll and, as if summoned by King Neptune, clouds of large brilliantly coloured butterflies made an aerial tapestry over and around the ship as the 'Bears' boarded.

They pursued everybody from Vice-Admiral Tennant (who produced documentary extenuating circumstance) and Captain Hughes-Hallett (who couldn't), down to the lowest rating of the lower deck and hauled them with mock screams to the wooden razor and ducking stool.

New Years Day was piped as an extended 'Make and Mend' except for the Royal Marine Band still voyaging as passengers who were pressed into giving a two-hour concert on the forecastle. There was a parody on Wagner's overture to Tannhauser, and Alan Dale acquitted himself well with what was called 'a rendition' of Love Could I But Only Tell Thee.

Another musical delight came my way a month later with a spur-of-the-moment bash on an upturned chair with a couple of spoons when I joined a trio of chaps bringing their instruments, a trumpeter, a clarinettist, and a guy with a guitar when an outbreak of polio necessitated fumigating Jamaica. The ship's company were put ashore, division by division, to sleep in grass huts, on grass beds, on a sandy beach, to swim in the early morning sea, sup the tot of rum beneath swaying coconut palms, and yarn till nightfall for five or six splendid days.

Then one day I overheard something in the mess that took me hot-foot to the Captain's Secretary. Years spent as a 'Small Ship Sailor' made me forget the usual procedure such as 'Request Men' and going by way of Petty Officer, Divisional

Officer et cetera... I tapped on his door.

'Come in'.

'Sir' I said, 'you are over complemented'.

What exactly do you mean by that signalman? And have you seen the Chief Yeoman?'

'No sir, I thought...'

He silenced me with a raised hand, 'First you must talk to your Yeoman of Signals, he will then make arrangements with me. Is that clear?' and he bent his head to his books, the interview over.

My relief had been onboard nine days, but grudgingly I had to agree and with a salute left his cabin. At this point in my memoirs I can say that I met this lieutenant fifty-six years later cruising a narrow boat on the Trent and Mersey Canal and he could remember nothing of the incident! However I was cast off the very next day when we got to Ceylon, at a dump called Bambara to await passage to England, where I saw frigates and sloops and destroyers come and go, until fourteen days later I got drafted as a passenger to an aircraft component ship called 'Holm Sound' with a full speed of nine knots. It was the 18th March 1946.

During the thirty-eight day voyage to Spithead the inept League of Nations held its last meeting, the last British troops vacated Syria on the 15th April, and policy-maker Bevin assured the House of Commons that the Russian-Persian oil agreement did not infringe our oil supplies from Persia...as far as could be seen.

At Spithead I disembarked to the strains of 'Rum and Coca-Cola' a song popularised by Carmen Miranda, The Ink Spots, and other small ensembles now called 'Groups'.

The journey from Portsmouth to Plymouth was most tedious and immediately on arrival at 'Guz' (H.M.S.Drake, Devonport), a Petty Officer directed me to make my way to the Demobilisation Centre at St. Budeaux. I was fair tuckered out by this time, the very idea of actually going to St.Budeaux raising such weird thoughts that the slow clack, clack, clack of wheels hitting rail joints must have sent me nodding off to sleep, and when I awoke to the porter's shout I hurriedly sprang to the platform and cried, "H.M.S.Impregnable, mate, how do I get there?'

He pointed with his flag, 'Down there young feller, end of that lane. You can't miss it'.

So I am going along expecting to see some water with a harbour holding warships when into view comes this huge gate flanked by stone structures supporting a barrier which lifts just as I reach it, and what I take to be a guard approaches with a terse, 'Yes?'

Putting down my suitcase I say, 'I've been called up. I've got a letter somewhere in me pocket telling me to report to H.M.S.Impregnable, this is it isn't it?'

Opening a small pedestrian gate I had not noticed and glancing at the badge I was wearing in the lapel of my jacket, proclaiming my membership of the Union of Post Office Workers, he smiles and says, 'Used to work for the 'Gyppo' me self once lad, and if you'll allow me to give you the best bit of advice you're ever likely to receive in this 'ere establishment it's this, don't take a swing at anybody calling you a bastard....it's a term of endearment in the Andrew'.

Standing about are half a dozen other young chaps silently appraising the situation and each other, soon herded together and walked to a store room to be given a kit-bag and a hammock. Next on the agenda is the drill-hall where about forty more recruits are trying to fix their hammocks to crossed metal rods. It takes twenty minutes or maybe half an hour to rig these contraptions to the satisfaction of the Petty Officer, then off we go for a late meal. It's getting dark. Am I sleeping? Am I dreaming?

It's light again. Early morning, sixish. I'm used to that back home, reveille will be no problem. The porridge might be though.

Kitting out is next and we're stamping our names and numbers (I've just been allocated mine, D/JX340782 onto every article of clothing ...the collars with the white bands denoting the victories of Lord Horatio Nelson look dreadfully new and I hear someone mention frequent dhobying...<u>dhobying</u>?

'Fall In!' Somehow we manage to get ourselves in ranks in front of a Naval Lieutenant and he is actually <u>welcoming</u> us to 'the ship' explaining that we shall be separated into two classes for instruction as signalmen, V67 and V68, that we shall be accommodated in Weymes Hut and sleep in bunk beds. A sigh goes up around me.

His place is taken by a Petty Officer and a three badge Leading Signalman calling out names from a clip-board: Stott, Jeffries, Walker, Pettit R, Pettit W, (twins these), Lee, Norman, Jones, Wilkins....and mustering at the side of the three badge killick march to the first lesson in the Morse code. where I hear him saying, 'Now first you must elect a class leader from among yourselves. His job will be to act as your spokesman to collect your 'nutty' and tobacco rations and to be my aide or my second arm when I'm away on leave'.

We look at one another, complete strangers, all of us. Who has the quality, the temerity, and the idiocy to volunteer? I do. Three steps forward and I'm nominated unanimously, presented with a red cloth anchor to be sewn to the left sleeve of my brand new jacket.

So begins the rigorous winter training period shivering on the bleak parade ground buffeted by the cold winds sweeping over a grey Western Channel. Reading a flickering light on the outside wall of the drill hall spitting out dots and dashes, raising bunting to yard-arm chocks on wet and icy halyards, waving semaphore flags with stiff fingers. In over-heated classrooms we sweat learning the intricacies of the Fleet Signal Book and the more accessible International Code of Signals.

The patience of the instructor and determination on our side are beginning to bear fruit as we approach the warmer months and as reward Lt.Cdr Fairie has agreed that some of us may take a whaler on the River Tamar and right now I'm rather desperate, feeling I've done the wrong thing. For we are stranded on the mud just below Saltash Bridge, the shore some two hundred yards distant. Yes, I realise our predicament has more of farce than tragedy, and sit in gloomy anticipation of unseemly ribaldry when returning to the rest of V.68 back at the Impregnable. The noon-day sun is inducing increasing sensations of thirst, already I have despatched two of our number to wade across the mud-flats to seek a public house or shop and to telephone the Impregnable to acquaint them with the reason for our delay. Watching those two ..er.. volunteers occasionally floundering thigh-deep in the oozy evil-smelling refuse of the hills I discover how lonely is the office of command, but hey! the water is rising! The tide's on its way in.

'Ted! Look!' Ronnie Pettit is pointing over my shoulder, 'there's a boat coming!'

'Well we don't need 'em now do we?' I say, 'let's get back by ourselves, right?' and the Commander has a hot meal and showers prepared for us when we get back.

When I am old I'm sure that I shall often remember this particular time as I stand at Sunday Divisions in front of my chums in the place of the Killick who has gone on week-end leave. The service is over; the inspection of ranks over, the band is beginning the Quick March to take the Parade past the Saluting Dais.

Swinging about, I face my class-mates, 'Right turn!' I order.; quick march, left, left, left right left,.... left wheel....'

The band is playing 'Heart of Oak Are Our Ships, Hearts Of Oak Are Our Men' and by gum, I'm believing it!... 'Into line, left turn! I hear the beat of drum matching our step...Class V.68...Eyes, right!' and I raise my right hand, I feel ten feet tall, and do I see a flicker in the eyes of the Commander as he returns my salute?

I have passed as Ordinary Signalman with recommendation for early advancement and my first draft has brought me to a Port War Signal Station in the Firth of Forth, a rocky and barren outcrop below the railway bridge spanning the water opposite Leith, my job to challenge all vessels coming up the firth. There are ten signal ratings here, supervised by a Lt.Cdr R.N.R. A squad of soldiers man the Battery.

I've found much is routine exchange signals, with trawlers and small coasters based at Leith and well acquainted with the twice daily alteration of these recognition signals, but here is the 'Rattler', a giant American 'Flat-top' squatting obliquely across my vision having totally disregarded my three challenges. 'Ted', says the Killick of the Watch, who calls everybody 'ted' except his superiors, 'I'm calling the commander to the bridge', and goes to the telephone bringing that worthy immediately who insists that I flash the vessel once again which again brings no response. 'Damn, I'll put a shot across her bows!' swore Lt.Cdr Smith winding up the blower to the Battery while I am quite looking forward to some fun of course. But time passes and 'Rattler' steams past above the submerged mine-field either oblivious or contemptuous of our intent. At the end of my watch I intend to go below to the mess where I am being taught Bezique by the older men. Reservists of course, called to this sinecure, which I feel, won't last much longer for me.

As if embroiled in a nightmare I am looking at the S.S.Drottingham and Empress of Russia steaming through the firth. Today is the 25th October 1943 and these Red Cross ships are carrying repatriated prisoners of war. Off-loaded at Leith, the band plays, the Lord Provost reads from a paper, the band swings into a cheerful chant while stretchers, the blind, the limping fumbling men are ambulanced to Waverley Railway Station and I get into the tender to take me back to my soft number on Inchkeith.

But because of recent advancement to full Signalman a draft chit is awaiting me there. I am to proceed to Londonderry and report to H.M.S.Columbine, a corvette.

My world was about to change. A sudden lurch and I was wrenched from sleep as the train fitfully puffed to a stop at St. Budeaux. Squaring my cap and tugging at my Number One's with its single gold stripe - three years of undetected crime- - I leapt from the compartment with far more alacrity than my earlier arrival on 'call-up' had occasioned, and it was no bother finding my way despite the fact that the station was now porter-less due to shortage of manpower, because although four years had gone by, the hedge-lined lane had not altered in any way its direction to the old training establishment H.M.S. Impregnable where I had passed out as Ordinary Signalman. I spent a few days there handing in my kit, signing papers which would keep me tied to a recall should emergency require, and wandering foot-loose around Plymouth Hoe where bumping into some of the men who had been boys with me in the Class of V.68, we exchanged personal histories. We had in fact come full circle to pick up a war gratuity of twenty-one pounds which of course on the 14th May 1946 was worth five thousand and forty of the larger type of penny.

I collected my bowler and returned to former occupation delivering letters to offices around Victoria Street and The Houses of Parliament.

As I write the finishing lines of this history on 1st March 2003, a call on my mobile tells me that my friend, Lt. Albert Baker one-time Keeper of the Queen's Cabin on the Royal Yacht 'Britannia', or more familiarly as Steward 'Bagsy' Baker of H.M.S. Columbine has recently died. An obituary appears in 'Navy News' but here is how I shall ever remember him:

In those days when Liverpool supported a seven mile long stretch of docks along the Mersey, and a troop of cart-horses to haul goods along Dock Road, members of Columbine's crew returning from a run ashore were staggered to see Bagsy sitting with his head in his hands and tears on his cheeks. The rough sailors immediately rebuked him for not being more circumspect with his intake of Liverpool ale.

'No,' sniffed our ship-mate, 'it isn't that. I sorta borrowed one of them Mersey Docks and Harbour Board nags for a mascot and the stupid thing wouldn't get up the gang-way and scarpered off down there somewhere too fast for me to catch him again.'

Lieutenant A. W. Baker, MVO.

Keeper and Steward

of the Royal Appartments,

Royal Yacht Britannia.

1953 - 1970

Addendum

Ldg. Tel. Eric Davis 'dipped' the exam for Commissioned Warrant and transferred to the seaman branch and many many years later I, with my wife and son, met him at a Scottish shore establishment shortly before retiring as a Master-at-Arms; he recorded on what he referred to as 'that devil machine' the following which I'm sure sums up what we all in Columbine ever felt:

I've been twenty-eight years in the Andrew and loved every minute of it.
I spend many hours reminiscing and casting my mind back a bit;
The memories I have keep me going. I could write a good book about them;
The ships and stone frigates I've served in, the companionship of the men.
But one ship stands out above others from those black days of the war.
And she was a flower class corvette, the Columbine - K.94.

T'was all fool's day '41 that I joined her In North Shields just 'ere she sailed.
I looked at the size of the vessel and I'm sure that I visibly paled.
I didn't think she'd ever make it across the Atlantic and back,
She looked just like a steel coffin; by golly the outlook was black.
I shouldered my kit bag and hammock and carried them over the prow
I felt my stomach was sinking and wished I hadn't joined now.
The crew only numbered but sixty, the communicators were ten,
They were made up of four sparkers, two coders, and four signalmen.
A motley collection of fellows, from all walks of life they had come,
But the spirit that bound them together was stronger than neat navy rum.
I suddenly felt a lot better; they looked a good crowd to me,

I soon had my head in a bucket; and found I wasn't so tough.
They welcomed me as a mess-mate, not as one on his first time at sea
We sailed on a convoy that evening, and blimey, wasn't it rough!
I couldn't have cared if the ship sank and inwardly called for my mum
The nausea didn't last long though, once I took charge of my tum..
During the four years that followed we had our moments of fear,
Intermingled with periods of pleasure; runs ashore our loved ones, beer
We all got to know each other, our failings - and attributes too;
Despite being a mixed bag of people, our comradeship carried us through.
We had to have understanding of the other chap's point of view
We had to think of not only ourselves but the rest of the crew.

The U-boats came out in their dozens; reconnaissance planes came as well,
Torpedoes were fired on occasion; for merchantmen it was sheer hell.
We did our best to deter them and keep them from sinking our ships,
For every loss that we suffered meant a further tightening of lips.

The vital sea-lanes were kept open; the food-stuffs we kept bringing in,
And all the time we were certain that we would eventually win.
The whole thing depended on team work, we carried no passengers then,
We worked as a fighting unit of sixty or so well trained men.
From signalmen manning the Aldiss, telegraphists glued to their 'phones,
Down to old 'Doc' in the sick-bay ready to splint broken bones.
From the stokers keeping her moving to seamen manning their guns
We all did our best to destroy them with our numerous depth-charge runs.

We can claim neither fame nor glory. We got no distinction as such
But if medals were given for effort then sixty would not be too much
Now that after two decades most have retired from the sea
And gone to their own occupations leaving, still serving - just me.

Let's remember those war-time companions who no longer live on this earth
Let's pray for their souls and revere them, for only we know their true worth
Now that I'm leaving the Service the happiest memory of mine is
The friendship of those who sailed with me in His Majesty's ship Columbine.

Eric Lionel Davis L/Tel. H.M.S. Columbine 1941 - 1945